THE ALCHEMY OF
TRANSFORMATION

THE ALCHEMY OF TRANSFORMATION

lee lozowick

Foreword by Claudio Naranjo, M.D.

Hohm Press
Prescott, Arizona
1996

Library of Congress Card #95-51641

Typesetting, Design and Layout:
Kim Johansen, *Black Dog Design*
Cover: Kim Johansen

HOHM PRESS
P.O. BOX 2501
PRESCOTT, AZ 86302
520-778-9189

For my Father, Yogi Ramsuratkumar,
He is the light by which I see,
the Heart through which I feel,
and the wisdom I one day
hope to realize.

Contents

Foreword

by Claudio Naranjo, M.D.

When I first saw Lee Lozowick's book, *In the Fire*, and read some paragraphs at the small IDHHB (Institute for the Development of the Harmonious Human Being, Inc., Nevada City, California) publishing company, I thought he might be one of Mr. Gold's creations (E.J. Gold is the director of the Institute, a widely published author on the subject of human transformation, and a recognized artist), and a pseudonym for one or another of Mr. Gold's alter egos. Lee and his "Hohm Foundation" (the company name under which the book *In the Fire* was published) were scarcely known then. By 1990, however, he was already well-known enough to deserve a chapter in Georg Feuerstein's book, *Holy Madness: The Shock Tactics and Radical Teachings of Crazy-Wise Adepts, Holy Fools, and Rascal Gurus*, (New York: Arkana/Penguin Books, 1990) among an array including Chogyam Trungpa, Da Love Ananda (formerly Bubba Free John, or Da Free John), George Gurdjieff and others. More recently, at the request of Lee's own guru, Yogi Ramsuratkumar, a chapter on Lee was included in *Facets of the Diamond* (Prescott, Arizona:

Hohm Press, 1995), a volume on the wisdom of India. I would not mention it had I not found the quoted passages of Lee Lozowick to be at least as interesting as those of his own guru, or those of Papa Ramdas, Shirdi Sai Baba and others.

I had occasion to get a glimpse of Lee Lozowick's work when I visited his ashram at the time of his community's April Fool's Celebration two years ago. Here I took part in a public discussion of issues of spiritual authority and crazy wisdom with Lee's disciples and with Dr. John Haule, Ph.D. (director of the Jung Institute at Chestnut Hill, Massachusetts). Since I had already listened to a recording of Lee's rock band—*liars, gods and beggars*—I was surprised to find that daily practice on the ashram included the traditional *Arati*, the *Guru Gita*, and other prayers that I had become acquainted with in my visits to Swami Muktananda's ashrams in the late 1970s. I already knew Lee to be in the tradition of *Guru Bhakta* — where devotion to the spiritual guide is emphasized as a vehicle—but only in the course of this visit could I see how he managed to be at the same time a God-man and an open, honest and humble human being. I was intrigued and impressed, and continued to learn from his example during a later visit to his Boulder, Colorado circle of students when Lee and I were both invited speakers at Naropa Institute's 2nd Annual Conference on Crazy Wisdom and Divine Madness.

I have read this manuscript, *The Alchemy of Transformation*, with a genuine interest in knowing more about how Lee teaches—more than my brief visits permitted. The transcripts of his German seminars, from which this book is made, and in which he precisely addresses this issue of how he teaches, has constituted a perfect opportunity.

Ever since, in the early 1960s, I read an essay by Rabindranath Tagore entitled *My Religion*, I wanted to know more about the Bauls; and when some ten years later the first recordings of Baul music appeared in the American market, I began to use them in my work on "consciousness through music" as a stimulus to a devotion permeated by eroticism. That Lee Lozowick (or Mr. Lee, or more formally, Mr. Lee Khépa Baul) is the devotee of an Indian God-Master and also uses music as an important part of the spiritual practice that he proposes, is, then, coherent with this most particular affinity between us. Yet, I do not imagine that it is only in view of a Baul-mindedness that I have been asked to write this Foreword, except in an inner sense of informality, spontaneity, originality, tolerance for madness, eroticism, humor, a keen sense of one's idiocy and the ambition of being a slave of God.

The other reason is that even while Mr. Lee is not a professional psychotherapist (and in spite of his, "I am not interested in your neurosis," to emphasize that his role is that of providing "God-connection"), his work is, as this book shows, an individual synthesis of spirituality and psychological house-cleaning not usually provided by traditional teachers and spiritual communities. He is one who transmits an Oriental teaching in a non-traditional Western manner, working at the edge of the psychotherapeutic domain. And, because I am one who started at the other end of things (first a psychotherapist and later one nourished by Oriental wisdom), it is fitting that I serve as his herald before the world of my colleagues and psychologically-minded readers.

I believe seekers will find his book of interest because of its freshness and because of what it makes explicit about working on oneself, relating to a teacher and being in a community.

I hope *The Alchemy of Transformation* may help seekers become better seekers, and help society understand its call to transformation, its work and its predicament.

Berkeley, California
April 1995

Introduction

by Regina Sara Ryan

The Baul is virtually unknown in the West. A 700-year history in the Bengal region of India is documented by few books, some scholarly articles, and a scattered collection of songs and poems. The picture which emerges from even a cursory study of these works is of a group of mad beggars and poets, a fierce and passionately devotional people—individualistic, iconoclastic, visionary, lusty, loving and free. All their practices, i.e., the use of breath and sex and song, are aimed at the awakening of the Heart, and to relationship with the "man of the Heart"—their description of the Divine Beloved who indwells in each being.

Bauls are typically wanderers, moving from village to village carrying only their instruments of song and praise. Dressed in the cast-off clothing of Hindus and Muslims alike, the Bauls defy custom and orthodoxy. Occasionally they gather in big fairs (melas) to celebrate together in song, and then as quickly as they appeared, disperse to roam the countryside once again.

"and the Bauls came
they danced
they sang
And they disappeared
in the mist..."[1]

A Baul lives the life of one who remains "wholly dedicated to his own nature. He laughs or cries, dances or begs as he wishes... a dancing beggar." [2] Yet, the Baul is a beggar who turns the conventional world upside down—shaking loose habits of mind and emotion, awakening his listener to the spontaneous essence of life.

This book is the chronicle of a series of seminars given by the American Baul, Lee Lozowick, in the Spring of 1988 as he travelled through Germany with a group of his friends and students. This contemporary Baul band, generally dressed quite simply and cleanly, roaming the country in a small caravan of VW vans and assorted passenger cars, bore little physical resemblance to their Bengali ancestors. Yet, for those fortunate enough to travel with Lee and attend his talks, the alignment in mood, texture, and theme to the traditional Baul bards was evident.

Lee would say (or do) almost anything to provoke his audience to attention. Only then, he reiterated in a score of different ways, was there a possibility to loosen the grip on righteousness and appropriateness that we held to for safety and self-definition in this chaotic universe. Only a shock or laughter (one of his favorite tools) offered the opportunity to drop one's guard, to relax the mind momentarily, and thereby allow for the possibility of penetration from within. . .the opportunity to remember what is always, already accomplished. . . to remember God. For it is a foundational principle of Lee Lozowick's teaching that, "God does not live in the sky." Rather, the Divine is to be found in the very breath that saturates our cells, the blood that swells our veins, and in the simplest and most ordinary functions of everyday existence.

Like the Baul songs, Lee's words are both poetic and irreverent, blending stories of the mystic's longing for the Divine with the raucous taunts and off-color jokes of the street-wise hustler. Like many Zen and Sufi Masters before him, this Baul Master, Lee Lozowick, will not be tamed! Attempt to press him into one box, or definition, and in his next sentence he leaps back with ferocity to contradict both himself and you.

Lee has referred to himself by many names: the Fool of God, the Arrogant Fool, the Beggar's Beggar, the Bad Poet, and each of these titles is confirmed as one reads the text of these lectures. His is not a new-age spirituality offering promises of enlightenment techniques and warm feelings. His teaching is rather a radical, traditional, elegant and irreverent presentation of a way of life, through surrender to the Guru, which leads to an alchemical transformation of the human being. It requires discipline, devotion, intentionality and practice. The casual reader is warned in advance that no easy answers are found here. To "play" with a Master is to play close to the edge of an abyss. One is advised to step cautiously, yet be prepared for a fall which can sometimes prove to be a rollicking, good time.

My own fall into this Master's Way began at the age of forty after a helter-skelter career of spiritual searching. On a path of extremes, I had already spent eight years as a semi-cloistered Roman Catholic nun and three more as a red-robed sannaysin of the controversial Bhagwan Shree Rajneesh, whom the media had sensationalized as the Sex-Guru. I had literally gone around the world and back in my eagerness to find "the pearl of great price." By the time I met Lee I was primed—skeptical, cautious, hungry, and longing ever more intensely for something Real. I couldn't quite anticipate what that would look or feel like, but I knew I had tasted it in rare moments throughout my life, and would hold it tight if it showed up again.

My initial encounters with the Master were dramatic only in the sense of the clarity and power of the inner resonance which occurred between us. Speaking with him for the first time, in a formal, public setting, I was plunged into a silence of mind and simultaneously experienced an enlivening of the heart. He spoke to the body in a way that I had come to recognize, from my previous work, as the gateway to a domain of worshipful gratitude in which I was not separate from anything, or anyone. There was the direct sensation of his voice coming from inside my own chest and belly, even though his physical body sat at a distance of at least thirty feet from me. And the compassion in his looks and words drew from me questions that I didn't know I had, and many, many tears.

In the years that have intervened since that initial meeting I continued my work as a college psychology teacher and professional writer and consultant, while moving steadily closer to the edge, closer to the Heart. Respect for this teacher's work grows in me. This Baul Master has interrupted my life with his vision, his music, and his everpresent intoxication for the Divine.

Lee Lozowick's work is subtle, and therefore easily missed by the casual observer. He is an alchemist—one involved in the business of transforming the baser metals into gold—the metaphor which most accurately describes his work with human beings. But, the way in which he accomplishes this subtle, even magical, process is so obviously simple and ordinary that it is often misinterpreted and overlooked. One of the best ways to hide something, it seems, is to put it out in the open and tell the plain truth about it.

And, his work is timed with excruciating precision, another aspect which drives away the seeker after instant results and dramatic experiences. "Time is the great tester" is a phrase he is most fond of using, and one that characterizes his work with his students and devotees. One doesn't so much study or learn his teaching. Rather, one absorbs it, or literally him—slowly, over time. It is this absorption which accomplishes the work of transformation, from the inside out.

It is a hallmark of the Baul culture that the thirsty lover of God will drink from any well where the water is pure. Drawing from a wide variety of sources both sacred and profane, Lee Lozowick speaks the language of contemporary Rock and Roll with the same ease with which he interprets Zen Buddhism, the writings of George Gurdjieff and other "4th Way" teachers, the poetry of the Sufi mystic, Rumi, the life of Jesus, and the teachings of Christian mystics and saints.

The necessity for immediate translation for his German audience slowed and focused Lee's more usual rambling style of presentation. The resulting lectures were extraordinary, in both concentration of content and intensity of mood. Even long-time students claimed that they had never heard the Master quite so clear and thorough in his explication of his teaching work.

It is a rare treasure—a roadmap of the spiritual path, and a guided commentary by one who has walked it himself. Beginning with an indication of what "the Work" of Transformation is, he goes on to explain how a Master works, using his own approach as a model. Later chapters concern the need for discipline and practice; the value of community in spiritual work and contemporary culture; a scathing commentary on sex, love and relationships; the use of "Enquiry" or rigorous, self-observation as a way of piercing the all-controlling mechanism of mind; and an elegant treatment of the nature of devotion in which he addresses the question of questions: "Devotion to what? Devotion to whom?"

Profound concepts are presented in a way that is deceptively simple and accessible, and the first-time reader is cautioned to let the words in with the heart as well as the eyes.

Traveling in Lee's company through a dozen German cities and towns over this intense six-week tour, I had the opportunity to scrutinize him under circumstances of chaos and tension, and in moments of relaxed camaraderie. What I saw was a revelation to me. Here was One who lived and breathed, in every moment, a singular intention—the awakening of humanity through the Alchemy of Transformation to its rightful place within the Great Process of Divine Evolution.

This book provides the reader with a similar opportunity for understanding, and for sharing the vision and benediction of this extraordinary individual, the Baul Master, Lee Lozowick. Let his words, like buoyant empty vessels, carry you, too, down this River to meet the Ocean—the Heart of the Divine.

"My heart is a lamp, moving in the current, drifting to some landing-place I do not know. Darkness moves before me on the river, it moves again behind, and in the moving darkness only ripple sounds are heard, for underneath the ripples moves the current of the quiet night. My lamp, as if to seek a friend, goes drifting by the shore. Both day and night my drifting lamp moves searching by the shore. My Friend is ocean to this river, my Friend is the shore to this shoreless river. The current bends again. At one such bending he will call to me and I will look upon his face, and he will catch me up in his embrace, and then my flame, my pain will be extinguished. And on his breast will be extinguished, in my joy, my flame." [3]

1 quoted by Raymond, Lizelle, To Live Within, Garden City, New York: Doubleday & Co., 1971, p. xxvi.
2 Bhattacharya, Deben, Songs of the Bards of Bengal, New York: Grove Press, Inc., 1969, p.23
3 Baul Gaṅgārām; quoted in Dimock, Edward C., Jr. The Place of the Hidden Moon {Chicago and London: University of Chicago Press, 1966}, p. 266 267.])

THE MAGICIAN'S SECRETS

A stage magician, one who is a Master of his art, will only tell his secrets to two kinds of people. He'll tell the pure curiosity seeker—the person who is either just making conversation, or whose curiosity is a habit ... The Master Magician knows this type of person will never seriously pursue magic and use the secrets, and in effect, telling something to this kind of person... is just like talking to a stone wall. Such people are harmless enough.

The second type of person such a Magician will reveal his secrets to is someone who is absolutely serious, absolutely interested in making real use of this Magic and who will be responsible, even obligated, for this very rare and important knowledge. Such a ... person will be more than happy to undergo whatever the Magician suggests, to enter into an often long and exhausting apprentice-ship, often spending a year or even more doing no more than car-rying bags and props, and sweeping floors or dusting boxes, before even knowing the most basic secrets. Such a person will value the Magician's knowledge at its true worth, and will be sure not to treat it frivolously or throw it around too cheaply. And such an apprentice will be sure to pass the secrets of the Master on in the same way, only to the same types of people, himself being careful to select only the most serious and devoted apprentice or apprentices.

All of the types of people between these two extremes become very dangerous "material" to deal with. There are some who seek only their own enrichment and will sell the secrets to the highest bidder or prostitute them in the common market place for money and fame. Others will spread the secrets randomly and widely, diluting the True Value of Magic as an Art and as a Way. Others will assume they know much more than the Master Magician and so will "modernize" or "upgrade" these tried and true, and most ancient, secrets with their own personalities, their own individual tendencies and eccentricities, thereby rendering the original Magic and original secrets all but undecipherable in a very short time. Some could conceivably even be lost forever in their True form. And some simply use these most rare and sanctified secrets as party games, raking them through the lowest of the low levels of culture (or lack of it) and completely destroying the Real communication or knowledge that they are meant to embody.

So the Master Magician is mindlessly applauded... by the first type, revered and gratefully accepted by the second type (with unspoken thanks, too sacred to be put into words), and ridiculed, cursed, defamed, or ignored, becoming the butt of jokes and the scapegoat of sarcasm and cynicism by all of the rest. But the Master Magician remains Master Magician despite the audiences, of any kind. This is his principle reason for existence, simply the actual manifestation of the Mastery itself. And the acceptance of an apprentice or apprentices (if he should ever be so lucky) is his obligation to his craft, his art, his knowledge.

I will leave the parallels that can be drawn to the Spiritual Master from the Magician up to the reader.

—*Lee Lozowick*

THE ALCHEMY OF
TRANSFORMATION

Chapter One

A MASTER WORKS

Let me begin with a gentle precaution. The way that I work is very personal, even intimate, so if my words provoke you a bit, try not to take offense. When I say that this way of working is very intimate I don't mean that I'm interested in anybody's private life or their business. I'm not at all interested in your relationships, your finances or your emotional problems. In fact, I am aggressively antagonistic to people who attempt to tell me about their personal lives. I don't want to know about them.

What interests me is that about you which is never out of communication with the Divine. But the unfortunate thing about us as individuals is this: What is never out of communication with the Divine is almost always out of communication with our faculty of attention. Thus the need for work. Spiritual work is not a quick answer to cleaning up the mess that our lives are in. Real spiritual work is never about what we can produce for ourselves, but rather what we can produce *out of ourselves* for something higher. The point of spiritual work is to serve God. If in serving God (and we'll have more to say about this later) the messes we have made of our lives clear up—great, wonderful. If the messes we have made of our lives do not clear up, and in fact get worse—well, blame God, go on, and keep working.

Spiritual work is about discipline and consistency, not necessarily about how beautiful and full of light things might look after you've been practicing meditation for a year or two. Actually meditation *will* transform your vision, but not before it clears out everything else that stands in the way. And that process may not be particularly attractive or comfortable. In fact, it may not even appear, or feel, sane.

A Master's work with students is like water. It will leave no space, no crevice, no little hidden pocket left untouched. Psychological and therapeutic work is often like trying to fill a space with stones. If you take a big stone and try to wedge it into a hole in the wall, what often happens is that the whole wall shakes and dust falls. It can be very dramatic, but still many fine cracks will be left unfilled. A tremendous number of life's aspects are left entirely untouched with these methodologies.

My work with people is intimate in the sense that it really gets in. It integrates in a way that's unusual for most kinds of transformative work—not unique, just unusual, and not necessarily rare if you know where to go.

I used to be a philatelist. I sold rare stamps. People would look at my inventory and say, "My God, where did you get so many rareties?," since to someone who was relatively naive it looked like the merchandise I had was extremely uncommon. Actually, because I was in the business, I knew where to go to find what I needed. I knew people who had ten times what I had, people who had vaults full of rare stamps. So too in this business of spiritual life. The work that I do is not unique. And it *is* hard to find. But if you know where to go, it's accessible. It's not secret work. It's only rare in the sense that most people don't find it, not in the sense that it isn't around; and it's rare because many others are unwilling or unable to pay the price for it (and I'm not talking about money).

My work with you might create a certain hunger for something that will be difficult to find. If that is so, I have done my job well. It makes no difference whether you become a student of mine or not. *Who* actually satisfies that hunger is not important. What is important is that the hunger gets satisfied.

We gave a seminar in Hanover recently, and at the conclusion I asked for questions or comments. One man was very simple and honest. He said: "I'm a bit angry and disturbed because something has been reenlivened in me that I've tried to forget. I have known a hunger for a type of 'food,' which I looked for in the past. But always when I got close to it I realized that it was going to be hard to come by. It meant too much, and since I wasn't willing to do the work necessary to get it, I pushed down and covered over my hunger for it. Now it's been years since I've even remembered it existed. But your talk has started these pangs again. I don't know if I like that. It's not something that really delights me. But I thank you anyway."

This man was honest. He admitted that he wasn't delighted at the prospect of re-enlivening that hunger. What gets touched by the subtlety of a Master's communication is not all goodness and light and purity. But once you connect with the passion, the mood and the life inherent in authentic teaching, you're liable to find yourself with an addiction that's very difficult to kick. I'm establishing the ground rules here so that you won't be too surprised. In my experience, however, I find that most people *do know* what they're getting themselves into when they begin spiritual work. Nonetheless, they're always surprised—sometimes pleasantly, sometimes not so pleasantly. But if we're afraid of surprises we'd better be forewarned because if this work takes hold in us there will be a lot of them.

It's very important for a Master to maintain a personal relationship with the student, to make sure that what is being touched is also being refined and perfected, if that's desired. It's like cutting a fine jewel. When someone cuts a diamond, he starts with this rough stone in it's matrix of dirt and other stone. First, the material must be cleaned, and the matrix removed. Then it must be tested to find any imperfections. Only then will the master craftsman know where and how to cut. He (or she) must decide what kind of cut the diamond will take—a pear cut, or a perfect cut, or a heart cut. When all of that is determined the work can begin. Still, with every tap of the hammer or every shave of the saw the diamond cutter has to stop and re-analyze the process to make sure that his original judgment was accurate. To facet a diamond is a very delicate and sensitive art, and not just anyone who has a stone tumbler that polishes agates can do it.

In my work with students, I cut diamonds; and I'm not willing to make one chip and then say, "Oh well, this is a nice diamond," and then just leave it. When I start something, I want to finish it. To do that requires direct attention.

Some teachers will say that all they have to do is just remember some student somewhere, and immediately grace, or God, moves out to take care of it all. My experience doesn't bear this out. When a teacher says that, what he (or she) usually means is that his connection to his student produces a lot of phenomena—even visions and other very powerful experiences. But I find that visions and experiences mean nothing if they're not integrated within an appropriate context. Even if one student has fifty cosmic experiences, that is irrelevant if the experiences aren't put into alignment in the correct way.

The value of a Master, the value of this kind of help, is not that the Master has wisdom to give you, since any of the traditional scriptures and contemporary books on Sufism, Buddhism or Gurdjieff work are full of wisdom. The Master's value is not that he or she knows something, but rather that he has the ability to bring into alignment what the student herself comes to know experientially. That's my domain of expertise—alignment. If I wanted to be sarcastic I would say that I'm just like a cosmic chiropractor. To make a better analogy, you might say that I'm like a structural engineer who tests stresses in a building. If the test is off a little bit and the building needs to be reinforced, or aligned, I'm the one who knows how to do that.

Since we're on a roll with analogies, let's try another one. I have often viewed this job I have as one of crafting a fine Samurai sword. The steel gets put into the oven in a very specific way, for an exact amount of time. Then it is taken out, tempered a bit, cooled, and then placed back in for another period of time. Then back out again, tempered, cooled, back in. . .and so on. This way of working with students is a very long and consistent process, and it is something which a Master does purely by instinct.

This Baul's way is not the Zen approach in which the teacher looks at you and says, "Just wake up! Just realize reality." Nor is it the approach of the Yogi who will say: "This is the truth! The heart is God. . .Well, why do you still have problems? The heart is God! Just live it—will ya?" I tried that approach in the beginning and I found that people thought they were doing that. Men would come to me and say, "I'm living the enlightened life. But my wife…you know, she just doesn't understand. I mean she just can't raise her consciousness, and I can't live with somebody like that." Well, that convinced me that they weren't living what they presumed to be living.

The whole issue connected with the term "enlightenment" is a loaded one. For me it became such a handicap that I decided it was just impossible to keep saying I was enlightened. I don't think I even know what enlightenment is. But what I *do* know is what resonates, and I know what is dissonant, and I know what is aligned or misaligned. So I can work with people, and I can help people refine and stay on track. That I know I can do. But enlightenment? Let's leave that to God. Maybe God knows something about that.

As we begin to deepen our explorations together, don't try to figure out exactly what goes on here except in the sense of having an innocent curiosity. And please do not base your feeling of success or lack of success in getting what I can offer or whether you have intellectually put all the pieces together or not. Rather, be willing to give some attention to what you *feel*.

So often, the communication of reality is simply the way you feel when you're around somebody—not on what he or she is doing or saying, or on how profound an artist he is. Rather, the communication is about who one is, not what titles one is known by. And, contrary to what you might expect, sometimes the least serious answers to your "serious" questions, are the most valuable. Which reminds me of a story.

There is a famous Zen story, a *koan*, about a very spontaneous teacher who came upon two of his monks arguing over a cat. The monks lived in different dormitories in the same monastery and each monk wanted the cat to be in his living quarters. Well, the teacher, Nanzen I believe it was, observed the whole situation in a moment. Walking up to the two monks who were pulling on this poor cat, he grabbed the cat and said to the monks, "Quick, tell me, is the flag flying because the wind is blowing, or is the wind blowing because the flag is flying? Answer now, or I'll cut the cat in half." The monks were so shocked by this that they were speechless. So Nanzen cut the cat in half.

Now if you know anything about the tradition of Buddhism, you know that, esssentially, it's a tradition of *ahimsa*, which is nonviolence. So, whether the practice of these two shocked monks was that of Zen Buddhism or any of the other forms of Buddhism, the essential principle of nonviolence was, and still is, true to all of them. Besides *ahimsa*, they would undoubtedly have assumed the Bodhisattva vow, which means they had pledged to save all sentient beings. . .not just the human variety. Such a tradition and such a vow certainly didn't allow for sending a cat to Nirvana by cutting it in half. The teacher's actions shocked them speechless—temporarily stopped their minds.

Often the catalysts that prove most effective in my working with students are catalysts which are not appreciable by rational intelligence. Yet, even if the mind cannot make sense from something, there is always a communication that the body realizes. Information is useful, but what is more useful is an instinctual feeling of what this Work is, and the willingness to be responsible to that—whether you understand it or not. Werner Erhard said, "Understanding is the booby prize." And I think he's right.

If you learn anything during our time together, what you learn will be the result of how clearly you're able to observe your experience, not whether you've had certain insights that you've never had before about points of spiritual practice. The way I work is not to patiently explain the answers to your questions so that you come to a kind of intellectual resolution. The way I work is to provoke experience, and then attempt either to define the experience so that *who* was provoked gets the definition, or just to hope that you're sensitive, intelligent enough, and have a deep enough intention to work on yourself that you get it on your own. Certainly you're all intelligent. There's no question about that. Unfortunately, intelligence is not a substitute for common sense or the willingness to be vulnerable or responsive, and that's what is necessary for any Master to work with you.

There's a story about an Indian Yogi who used to meditate for very long periods of time. For days at a time this guy would be in a state of *samadhi*, which is a kind of ecstasy. Well, one day while he was busily studying one of the scriptures, he casually asked his wife what she was making for dinner, to which she replied: "Your favorite, *samosas*." He was so pleased. Just before dinner he decided to meditate for a while, and as often happened, he went into *samadhi*. But this time he stayed in this state of bliss for fifteen years. His hair grew. His fingernails grew, and he probably peed on his meditation cushion. (You notice how these stories never explain about that part of it?)

Anyway, after fifteen years the Yogi came out of his *samadhi*. As soon as he regained normal consciousness he yelled for his wife: "Woman, where are the *samosas*?" She patiently explained to him that all of his years of spiritual practice and sacrifice and meditation didn't even make him a reasonable man. It was such a great shock for this Yogi to realize that his wife was right—his stomach was more important than all the spiritual experiences he'd had his whole life—that he became her devotee, her student.

The experience that I tend to provoke is not the experience of sacred communion or *samadhi*, as much as it is stark clarity of observation about who you are now. It's easy enough to generate some feeling of bliss or lightness in a room full of people who are supposedly working spiritually. It's even easy to generate ecstasy. But then, a few good beers, the right partner, and the Rolling Stones music for an evening can do that too. Ecstatic or pleasurable experiences by themselves are not transformational. They need to be integrated, digested and reanimated in a particular way in order to be useful. That requires work—i.e., practice.

Great insights are not transformational, in and of themselves, either. For instance, you may realize, through attending some workshop, or reading some book, that all you ever wanted to do was have sex with your mother. And this realization might endure for the rest of your life. But still, you have not discovered anything real about yourself. On the other hand, you may realize that you are a being of light. . .pure, flawless, a part of God, all of it. You might have other kinds of profound realizations that can't even be spoken about. It doesn't matter. Listen! First things first! It may well be true that you're *not* separate from God and that you *are* one of the cells in the Great Body of the Divine. But if your behavior in every moment does not serve that Reality, then the truth of it is essentially irrelevant. If you are in a supermarket when someone drops a bag of groceries on the floor and you don't help that person pick things up, what difference does it make how deeply you know you're a being of God?

Often a master's way of working is intentionally dramatic. I will sometimes exaggerate certain forms of behavior just to weed out people who are unwilling to show a little consistency in their desire to approach this work. When I do that in a way that offends someone's personal prejudices, or even repulses them, they are likely to take it too seriously, and that's a mistake. Say, for instance, I leap up in the middle of the room and look at all the mothers and start screaming, "You have crippled your children, for God's sake! When are you going to realize that?" Immediately, they start to defend themselves, "How can you say that. . .don't you know I really love my child. . ." and "Nah, nah, nah, nah. . . ," like that. Yet in their process of self-defense they may miss a very important opportunity for self-observation.

Sometimes my dramatizations are other than tirades. Years ago, for example, I was walking with some friends in the lower east side of Manhattan. There was a big pile of garbage on the sidewalk with this old mattress covering it. Now that mattress was pretty awful looking—ripped and dirty. So I said: "That looks like a nice place to rest," and was just about to fall onto it when two of the women who were walking on either side, grabbed me with grips of steel. "Oh my God," they practically screamed, "that mattress has probably got every kind of disease imaginable. It's disgusting. It's filthy. It's. . .ugh." Get the point? In essence, that was a dramatization of people's relationship to dirt and disease. The way I look at it, most of you have probably slept on mattresses that have held more psychic dirt (which is infinitely more powerful) than any of the biological germs you might have picked up. Yes?

Instead of generating all sorts of tests and exercises for a student to work with, I take a more conservative approach. I like to wait for the environment to create the circumstance, and then I capitalize on the opportunity that the environment has already created.

Several years ago we travelled to India with about twenty-one people —seventeen adults and four children. Before leaving I had explained to the group that, rather than using Western-style hotels, it was my preference to stay in accomodations which the Indians themselves would generally use when they travelled. I also preferred to take buses rather than private cars, and to go with just the clothes on my back. At first everybody was excited for all of that. "Yeah," they said. "What a great adventure." But even though many of them had grown up in ghettoes in the U.S., and been on the streets of New York and Detroit, nothing prepared them for the streets of India. It was a great shock when we first walked into the hotel room in which we were to stay for several days. People looked around with disbelief. For some of them, especially the women with children, there was a wave of panic, "Oh no, what have I done in coming here? Are we ever going to get out of here alive?" It's not that I deliberately tried to make things uncomfortable and confrontive for people. Traveling itself did that, which is why it is very useful to the way I work.

This type of teaching work is not aimed at telling people what they don't know, but rather at revealing to them the dissonance of their present activity. This work is revelatory, meaning that it provides enough self-observation "food" for years of preliminary spiritual work. What a teacher does, and what the context of a spiritual school does, is to take your usual ego strategies (all the ways you deny and avoid the clarity of who you are) and stop you right in front of them. For instance, the first time I was ever in Germany I was in a room with a group of therapists. I deliberately made a vicious remark about Nazis, with a cruel sneer on my face, and a cold, judgmental tone in my voice. Everything stopped. Momentarily everybody in the room went into shock, and then a few started to cry, while others were becoming highly agitated.

"Wait a minute," one woman said, "Stop."

So I stopped.

She continued, "It's not that we don't want to hear what you have to say, it's just that we're not used to being talked to in this way. You have to understand this about us."

"That's exactly the point of why I said what I said," I responded. "A cultural dynamic (like you describe in excusing yourself) is the result of a certain kind of ego structure. It can't be excused just by saying: 'Oh well, that's just the way we are. . .have some patience with us. . .that's the way we are. . . .' Do you ever want to be any different?" I asked.

Heads nodded in agreement. By this time things had calmed down quite a bit, and I had changed the tone of my voice.

"To run away from things that either are uncomfortable, or just too big to handle, will never accomplish the transformation you are asking for," I explained. "You are just putting it off. You'll always be Germans. I'll always be an American. The French will always be French. The Russians will always be Russian, and those very cultural distinctions the languages, the art, the various moods are what make life interesting. But the neurotic disposition of any given culture, just like the neurotic disposition of any individual within that culture, cannot live in the same space as transformation work."

And the discussion went on from there.

One of my favorite sayings is, Time is the great tester. A lot of students have the idea that the teacher tests them to see if they're good students, or worthy students, but actually human psychology is so impatient and so variable that time is really one of the greatest testers, beyond anything that a teacher or a spiritual master could do. If people's tendencies to be distracted and to always look for immediate gratification are stronger than their desire for the teaching, or for this work, then they weed themselves out without my having to do anything. They become frustrated, and develop doubt in the master's ability to give anything. The saga of Marpa and Milarepa speaks to this point.

Marpa was a great Buddhist teacher who had a great student named Milarepa (who became a master in his own right). In the beginning, Milarepa was a powerful, dark magician who only wanted more power. He sought out those who could give him this kind of teaching, and if anybody refused him what he wanted, he would use his power to destroy them—kill them, or make them sick, or take all their money.

One day while Milarepa was off in the countryside doing magic, his mother died. When he learned of this he was thrown into a state of profound sorrow, because he loved her and had no other family. In his pain he realized that all his magic and everything he'd learned was of no value. Nothing was able to relieve the sorrow he was feeling. There and then Milarepa came to the conclusion that he needed to find another type of teaching.

Thus began a very long and arduous journey in which Milarepa asked everyone he met for recommendations of a good teacher.

Many people suggested he find a man named Marpa who lived in Tibet, so Milarepa journeyed there and asked Marpa if he could become his student.

Marpa's reply was, "Well, I'm not sure if you can be my student or not, but I need a house built and maybe you could build it for me. I'll watch you, and determine whether or not you are good material."

Milarepa set to work to build the house, by hand, with large stones. He soon became exhausted. Noticing this, Marpa would send his wife out with a little bit of rice gruel, and some water. "I'm a very poor man," Marpa would tell the student, "and I don't have much food to offer you. But this should be enough to fill your stomach."

It barely did, and rather quickly, Milarepa began to lose weight, and get very weak. But he kept on working. Just as the house was almost finished, Marpa arrived to look it over and appeared very upset.

"Oh, I've made a terrible mistake," Marpa said to the exhausted Milarepa. "I've asked you to build the house in the wrong spot. Please dismantle it and move the stones to the other corner of this field, and put the house up there."

Now to make a very long story short, the same thing happened a number of times for fifteen years.

Marpa kept saying to Milarepa, "Oh, I must have been drunk when I told you to do it there." He made every kind of excuse. He kept asking Milarepa to take down the house and rebuild it in a different place, or in a different style, or something. Milarepa got so weak that his bones were breaking, and occasionally he'd become so angry that he'd throw down the stones and start to leave, saying, "I just can't do it anymore; I've done enough. What is the teacher waiting for?"

Whenever that happened, Marpa would genuinely weep at the pain his student was enduring, but more so because he knew that the training process couldn't be stopped too soon.

Marpa's wife (thank God for women and their "devious" ways) was so moved by Milarepa's dedication that she would leave the house in the middle of the night when the master was asleep and bring additional food to Milarepa. "Keep going," she would assure him. "It's almost done. Just stick with it. I just know he's about to give you the teaching. Don't give up now."

And so Milarepa would stay. After fifteen years Marpa did give Milarepa the teaching—a particular form of meditation. Then he sent him away to a cave in the mountains to meditate for a few years, which Milarepa did. He meditated as his teacher had instructed him and ate nothing but nettles (since food was unavailable there) so that eventually his skin turned green. Eventually, Milarepa realized the fruits of his meditation completely, and Marpa, affirming that, simply said, "You don't need me anymore. Go and teach and communicate." So Milarepa did.

Years ago, I was talking to a Tibetan lama, named Geshe Wangyal. He was a very old, wise, and highly respected man (he is no longer living). At the time I had only been teaching for a couple of months and he'd been teaching for thirty years, so I wanted to know how my work with students would progress.

I asked him, "Do you have any students like Milarepa?"

Well, he started laughing, hysterically, and then he started coughing. His students, I'm sure, were afraid their teacher was going to have a heart attack. He laughed and coughed for a while longer, and then wiped a tear from his eye, got very serious and said to me, "This is 1975. There are no Milarepa's these days!"

It is through no fault of our own that we happen to show up at this time in history, in this place, and to be trained by our upbringing to be impatient and to always want self-gratification. It isn't our fault that we are generally unwilling to pay for what is of real value, and instead spend phenomenal sums on things of no real worth. (Recently, for example, in the United States, following the death of Andy Warwhol, there was an auction of his collection of cookie jars. They were estimated to be worth about $15,000, yet in auction they sold for about $115,000 just because they were Andy Warhol's cookie jars.)

While I value this story of Marpa and Milarepa tremendously, the kind I work I do with people is not the kind of work that Marpa did. It is not because I don't recognize what people need or how valuable that kind of effort would be. Rather, because we, myself included, are not willing to give the value to this work that it really has. The psychology of the culture-at-large is so twisted that most of the people who go to a Sylvester Stallone movie leave it feeling good, because in their fantasy identification they have lived out the role of some great hero. They actually believe that they can make life work just because they feel bolstered up, in a certain psychological way. Now they're Rambo!

Marpa gave Milarepa exercises to do for fifteen years. I let time eliminate those who are impatient, and unwilling to pay for the teaching with even a minimum of time and energy.

Perhaps at this point you can begin to appreciate that my purpose is to irritate you. If you leave here happy I will feel that I have done something wrong. But of course there's a difference between being happy and being satisfied. So I would like you to leave satisfied, but that won't necessarily mean happy. In fact, if you really understand what I am talking about you may be satisfied but very unhappy. The Work I represent does not give you the possibility of doing whatever you want. The Work that I represent, essentially, is work that eliminates your options, not work that gives you more of them.

Chapter Two

WHAT IS THIS WORK?

When people get involved in self development they often think that by becoming more conscious they'll have more options in life. Actually there are no such things as options. Either one is run by ego mechanicalness (in which case "you" are not choosing the options, your programming is), or else one is moved by the Will of God, and "you" don't make choices in this domain either.

Still, you probably think that you have some choices in your lives—like who to have a relationship with, what kind of job to take, what food you prefer and what smells attract you and repel you ... that kind of thing. Psychologically speaking, however, it can be proven that every choice you have ever made is based on unconscious factors that control you as effectively as the power of gravity controls you when you jump out of an airplane without a parachute.

You may think that the way you currently live is already pretty extraordinary because you can freely moan, or even scream, during sex, or you can sigh when you look at a work of Michelangelo, but that's all completely mechanical too. Just because a tear comes to your eye when you listen to Bach or Chopin or Mozart doesn't mean you can recognize art. The mind has the ability to mimic emotions so perfectly that you might swear that what you're experiencing is emotional when really it's just an intellectual simulation.

The work that I represent offers one the possibility to function in relationship to the Will of God—that universal energy that is always perfectly aligned with the momentum or evolution of all of creation—instead of from the mechanicalness of ego. Consequently, this work demands a revolution in your mind. Only one whose mind is no longer the autonomous, controlling factor of their entire conscious existence would dare to take on what the Buddhists call the Bodhisattva Vow—the oath to save all sentient beings before one saves oneself. (By the way, I know a lot of men who say they would like to save all the women in the world.... Which reminds me of a cartoon I saw recently in an American paper. Two women were talking and one said to the other, "You know, the more I find out about men, the more I like my dog." So, a lot of men would like to save all women, and a lot of women would just like to have good dogs. Well, now that you've gotten an idea of my sense of humor let's get on to something more serious.)

The first problem with the Bodhisattva vow is that essentially we're selfish. We might be willing to save a few sentient beings if there were something in it for us. But all humankind? We're not that interested. The second problem is that the only thing that would really inspire us to save sentient beings is if we felt their pain, and to most people that is an absolutely ridiculous consideration. I mean, don't we have enough of our own? We have our spouses, we have our children, we have our dying parents, we have work with emotional cripples everywhere, whether we are therapists or not. Our lives are already very full of suffering due to our relationships. The physical body is a source of suffering too. We get sick and become weak and tired at certain times. Then there's the variety of suffering that happens when we lose our concentration. There's the personal disappointment we feel at the unwillingness of the rest of the world to live the way we think they should live. This is a serious and continual suffering. So to consider taking on or feeling the sufferings of others is a thought that is beyond most of us, especially when you consider that these others will probably have lives that are much less peaceful or healthy than your own life currently is. There is a saying in English, "Who in their right mind would do something like that?" And that is exactly the point. No one in their "right" mind would do anything like that, ever! That's why to consider this Work you need a revolution in the mind.

If you turn your back on this Work you turn your back on humanity, and actually on life itself. But then again, most of us have our backs turned on life anyway, we just don't realize it. That in itself is a pretty dramatic realization when you get it. Imagine, all of our lives, our passions, our loves, our inspirations, our ideals have all been completely mechanical. Some people in relationships mechanically agree to fight regularly, and some people mechanically agree to get along quite well with one another regularly. Either way mechanicalness is mechanicalness. When you find that out, it won't necessarily mean that you'll look at your husband or wife and say, "Oh my God, I've made the wrong choice." Or you'll turn to your dog and say, "Oh God, not an Irish setter. How could I have done such a thing?" No. To realize your mechanicalness actually means that you have a chance to break through it. At last your relationship to those in your environment might just hold the possibility of being based on truth and reality, rather than simply on mechanical agreement.

This Work is not to be taken lightly, and I'll probably continue to warn you about this many more times. You may think that a warning like this is just my style, and that perhaps I'm using some kind of psychological technique on you, but I mean the warning seriously. Once you get into this Work to a particular depth, to the point that you really can't turn your back on life anymore if you try to, it will destroy you. So be warned.

One of the goals of this Work is the transformation of a human being from one who is capable of many levels of serious violence, to someone who is incapable of any abuses against life. That transformation is no easy job. Working with people over the last eighteen years I have noticed that most of us would be horrified to realize how easily the right trigger might provoke us. A lot of men, for example, believe that they're incapable of violence, especially physical violence toward women. Even the thought of it is enough to make them ill. And yet, take that same man and put him in the "right" circumstance with the "wrong" woman for enough time, and he's very likely to find out that, deep down inside somewhere, he's an extremely violent person.

As long as we're functioning mechanically, violently, ruled by our psychological dynamics, we can't produce for anything higher—which is what real spiritual Work is about. Even if you work in a hospital, ostensibly serving others, if you're functioning from a state of consciousness that is limited by mechanicalness, it's literally impossible to serve anything higher. No real Work begins until you are free of mechanicalness. Enlightenment is not the end at all. It is only the beginning. Without personal transformation it is impossible to serve one another because we are simply too selfish.

Most people can easily admit that the most fulfilling experiences of their lives have been when they were not conscious of themselves as isolated or separate entities. For instance, you are walking through a park and you see a couple of children playing, and in watching the freedom and innocence of the children you forget yourself. Only when you begin to remember yourself again will you realize how ecstatic or joyful you were in watching those children. Paradoxically however, we fight to maintain a sense of independent isolation when intellectually we know how much pain that provides, and how much ecstasy is present when we're outside of the sense of subject-object relationship. . .when we are momentarily without a rigid self-definition. This Work, then, is about submitting all that you define yourself as, to that which we define as God, but which in actuality can't be given a definition, or boundary. It cannot be analyzed.

The question then arises: How do you know that you're submitting yourself to God and not to some giant ego? I believe that every one of you knows when the raw truth hits—but few are willing to act on it or take responsibility for it because it is just too difficult. Every human being instinctually knows when his or her life is completely aligned with the energy that is universal. But most of us are able to override our feelings of dissonance because to act on that alignment is first of all shattering, secondly, it is heartbreaking, and thirdly it puts one in a position of being really alone. We're actually willing to deny the truth and to curse God by our refusal to recognize alignment.

After a while this denial becomes a habit and we don't even know we're doing it any more. Not only do we deny that we know the truth, but we start asserting that we're doing fine, we're perfectly aligned. . .etc. Our feeling sensitivity has become dulled. Suppose, for example, someone comes up to you in the street and says, "That's the ugliest shirt I've ever seen. Where did you get it?" Most of us, particularly the men, would probably believe that they were *feeling* something—anger, insult, offense, whatever. More likely, you would be using your superficial, "emotional" response to mask the dullness of your perception of what you were really feeling. I contend that we literally train ourselves, subconsciously, to have strong reactions to things in order to hide the fact that we really don't have any reactions at all. We really don't care.

Face it, we are dulled out, uncaring and selfish! When people begin this Work they may have the highest ideals. They say they want "to serve God," to "help mankind," to " be a Bodhisattva and eliminate suffering." But the bottom line is that we are suffering and we don't want to suffer. We begin this Work for our own purposes, to eliminate our own suffering, whether we think we do or not. But the good news is, if we stick to this Work long enough, through enough transformative crises, we just may end up serving God. (Do you believe me? You shouldn't. I have found that having to deal with people relating to me solely from a position of belief is much too difficult a task. Rely instead upon your own intuitive sense of rightness about what I say. To begin this Work requires a certain kind of instinctual realization.)

It is my contention that everybody *can* do this Work physically, but their minds won't let them. They don't have the psychological disposition required. A lot of what it takes is just to be stubborn enough to remember the first "hit" you got—like when you first heard the teaching spoken to you—in the face of all the doubts and confusion and conflicts that are bound to arise as the work progresses. If you appreciate the Work that is offered here, and begin to involve yourself in it, a literal, physical, cellular transformation will take place. But remember, when a caterpillar becomes a butterfly, the transformation may be natural, and ordinary, and graceful, but it's not untraumatic. Even a healing crisis that's ultimately health-producing is traumatic in some sense.

Trauma, as I use it here, describes a certain energy dynamic, and doesn't necessarily have a negative connotation. Years ago when I was Rolfed (a form of deep-tissue bodywork which can be very painful), there was a man in the room next to me who always had appointments at the same time I did. Every week I'd go in and lay down on the table for my treatment, and sure enough the guy in the next room would start screaming and yelling. It was the noisiest thing you can imagine. My Rolfer used to say that was "The Rolfer's Anthem." The process was definitely traumatic, but the result of all that screaming was a certain kind of freedom for the person being Rolfed. So too in spiritual Work. I won't promise you work that's free of crisis, or trauma, or serious difficulties once in awhile. It doesn't matter what particular path you take. If you are with a real teacher the path not only has some pitfalls, but some genuine difficulties. Then again, it's the only Work in the world worth doing anyway.

This Work is not about trying to make people over into some kind of passionless, nameless, faceless, always-wearing-the-same-kind-of-clothing, always-thinking-the-same-thing kind of non-entities. The Work that I represent is about getting people, any way I can—by seduction, threats, trickery, it doesn't make any difference what I use—to be the unique individuals that they are, from a position of clarity and freedom, rather than from a position of neurosis and weakness. There is no easy way to make that transition, however. There will be moments that are extremely unpleasant, and I don't like them any more than you do. But then if one wants the most that one can have out of this life, one pays the price and that's the way it is.

In Munich someone asked if it was necessary to "give up the world" in order to do spiritual Work, and I said no. It's not that you have to give up your precious possessions, or your personal vanity, even. What you have to give up is your present relationship to those things—possessions, vanity, whatever. Look at most of the Christian saints, for example. Look at St. Francis of Assisi and St. Thérèse of Liseaux. Now there are two people who in this day and age would be considered psychotic without any questions asked. Nevertheless, their serious clinical imbalance did not stop them from developing a very profound relationship to God. One of the difficulties of really coming to terms with transformation is that the elements of one's life don't necessarily change. Someone who's feeling the experience of transformation isn't necessarily levitating, moving through walls, or stopping bullets with his bare hands.

Years ago, our community in Arizona formed a softball team and we entered the lowest possible league in our town, the league with the very worst players. And this team was led by "Mr. Transformation" himself, me! In three years of playing the game we had a perfect record. We didn't win a single game. The interesting thing was, however, we started to develop a real fan club in the town because of our attitude toward losing. People would have so much fun watching us that they started to come around whenever we played. We would lose with scores of 35 to 2, and we would laugh, and pat one another on the back, "Hey, hey, made another ten innings with no score. . .ha,ha."

Transformation in our case didn't make us better softball players. It gave us a certain ability to act in an unpredictable way about having our faces smeared in the mud every time we played. I'm referring to our pride of course—not our physical faces. Transformation happens in action, in activity. It is not a passive or static state like *samadhi* or *satori* which are not transformative in and of themselves. What is transformative is the work that you begin to do, or the life that you begin to lead, based on the inspiration of these states of bliss or nonduality. God gets served in the midst of who you are and what you're becoming as a human being —in the midst of your struggles, your neuroses, your fears, your joys, your passions—not from denying or standing apart from your humanness.

In many different traditions reference is made to "dying before you die." St. Paul of Tarsus mentions this, and in the Sufi tradition there is a consideration about dying in life. Among other things, this refers to the ability to be different than an ordinary human being while still embodied in ordinary human form, but not because of some metaphysical desire to transcend distasteful stimuli. The transformation process that we engage in this Work turns us from purely biological or chemical factories into alchemical laboratories. For instance, instead of simply being able to transform unusable material into shit, which the body does naturally, we become capable of changing one substance into a substance of a completely different domain. Nisargadatta Maharaj, an Indian sage, said, "Psychotherapy can make a good ego out of a bad ego, but it can never do anything about the ego structure itself." That would require a kind of alchemy. The ancient and contemporary alchemists use the metaphor of changing iron into gold to describe this process.

When someone meditates, the subtle effects of that meditation literally affect the entire atmosphere of the earth. That's a form of alchemy that can have very significant repercussions. So, Bach and Mozart and Chopin probably didn't sit down and meditate to get their music, but where their art came from is the same domain that people access when they meditate. There's a power to the Masses of Bach, a power to the sculptures of Rodin and the paintings of El Greco, and there's infinitely more power to the artists themselves. A human being who develops himself in a particular way, an alchemically transformed human being, becomes a living work of art. This living creation, like Ramana Maharshi, before he died, or the Karmarpa, before he died, or Suzuki Roshi, before he died, effectively communicates far beyond the relative domain of the earth. I don't mean "far beyond" in the sense of distance like light years, but in terms of interspatial or interdimensional communication. The alchemy of consciousness, which is transformation, changes the context from one of "self" to one of "no self." That doesn't mean nonexistence or lack of consciousness. It means that one functions as an integral element in their environment rather than as an element that is always confronting the environment with some need to compete or establish separation.

The school and the teaching Work I represent is literally transformative—in the way that the Karmapa was a transformed being and in the way Ramana Maharshi and Suzuki Roshi were transformed beings. This process is effective over time to anyone who honestly engages it, and it is not linear—not a predictable "Step 1, Step 2, Step 3." The intricacy of our makeup and the relationship of all of the elements of our being are much too complicated for any linear process to be entirely effective. Nonetheless, there are certain functions, certain conditions, which I recommend, that dispose one towards transformation. Meditation, study, exercise, a vegetarian diet, a way of considering relationships—these orient us in the right direction, but they do not produce linear results. We don't meditate to get somewhere. We meditate to create a certain vulnerability, a certain openness, a certain receptivity; and the same is true of all of the recommended conditions of this school.

✝ ✝ ✝

The expression of discipline is not antagonistic to, nor does it exclude, a life that is fluid as a response to the Will of God. Rather, discipline and structure are a kind of matrix in which this spontaneity shows up. Thomas Merton, for example, was a member of the Trappists, an order of cloistered monks which is extremely strict in terms of ascetic lifestyle. Merton said that monks were in the monastery to celebrate God, and that there was always great humor and enjoyment of one another's company, even though most of their time spent together was in silence. This Work is not so much about getting *to* God as allowing the Will of God to become active. The strategies of ego—our mechanicalness, our perspective on life, our attitude of duality—are all effective shields that do not allow the Will of God to enter our being. Yet the benediction of God is always "on," always active. We don't need to somehow earn it, to climb a ladder to get it. All we need to do is to make the space for it to show up, that is, become receptive to what is always already moving and working and active. Paradoxically, the fact that this can take a long time, even a lifetime, is part of the lesson of the futility of ego's attempt to successfully achieve what it thinks it is achieving.

In the beginning of my work most of the people in the school were in their early twenties. When someone who was forty-five would come to the school and immediately connect with the Work, they'd say to me, "I don't have a problem with you. I know that you're doing something real. But this community! These people are so immature. They have such bad habits. I just cannot stay around because of all the people here." But they had missed the point. It's not that this Work demands that we eliminate every bad habit and every neurosis and every dissonant element of our personality, because that would take all our energy and maybe our whole lives too, and might not mean anything anyway. The point is that if we move into surrender to the Will of God, things that aren't necessary to serve that Will just won't show up, that's all. To work on bad habits is fine, but then again if serving God becomes more predominant, our bad habits will disappear by themselves without our doing anything about them.

We are born, we grow, we find ourselves reacting mechanically, and we find ourselves being attracted to Work that suggests that we can function non-mechanically. There is a law called the Law of Accident which refers to the fact that despite all our programming for mechanicality, there are times in which a person actually functions non-mechanically. When that impossible thing does happen, then you have Creation, and God is really attracted by Creation. In fact, all evolution moves towards Creation. Every element of Creation has varying possibilities for new Creation out of itself. Human beings, however, have the possibility of Creation all throughout their lives, many times. And that is what this Work is about, in practical terms.

26

Chapter Three

ABOUT SPIRITUAL PRACTICE,
AND PRACTICES

This Work is hard. It takes a lot to do it—particularly emotionally. You shouldn't be a martyr, but there are times in which you'll
have to bring heroism to it. It is common sense, therefore, to optimize the body's ability to process all of the considerations of this
Work. Spiritual practices, like diet, meditation, study, exercise,
monogamous sexuality, and other recommended conditions, do
that.

The practices are not processes to do so that you will get enlight-
ened. Enlightenment is not the issue. Serving God is the issue.
Utilizing the different practices establishes your ability to do this
Work, i.e. to serve God, most easefully.

For the body to utilize any transformative experience a certain
organic matrix (like a form or container) must be established to
hold the experience. This applies to mystical revelation, or a vision,
or the experience of sorrow or remorse generated by compassion
itself. In one sense the body is just like a big processing plant in

which things come and go and come and go. Sometimes, however, things don't move through and something sticks. Young children, for instance, have very pure digestive systems. Their bodies just take what is needed from whatever they ingest, and the rest is simply eliminated. But as we grow and eat things that are full of impurities and poisons, we actually coat the digestive system thoroughly. By the time we're adults it is not uncommon that the body cannot digest food properly at all. We have to take vitamins, enzymes, minerals, supplements and every other kind of thing to give the body what it is incapable of getting from our food.

It is the same story when you consider the "food" we obtain by transformational experiences. Most adults have developed to the point where they have obscured the natural matrix of the body. They cannot hold transformation due to the effects of ego strategies and the motivations of desire. It is not so much that they need to build a matrix that they don't have, as much as they need to eliminate the elements that have obscured or coated the matrix. This is precisely what practice does.

Practice is a kind of constant attention to what is dissonant, to what is restricting transformation from being held and used. It works from the inside out, and there is really no way to speed it up. You *just practice,* and at a certain point the body will be less obstructed and more able to hold transformative experience. It's not linear. With practice, transformation begins to evidence itself, but you can't trace it back to point out exactly where it came from. You can't credit it to "this meditation" or "that type of study." It just starts showing up. For instance, you may be reading the scriptures or a piece of poetry, and all of a sudden, swooooosh—a huge opening occurs within you, like you've been swept through a door that was never there before. Now you understand in a whole new way. That reading doesn't stand alone as "the" element which threw you into the opening. It was simply the catalyst, the final piece in a whole puzzle that was being put together. Practice is like the outline and the frame of the puzzle.

Food and Diet

Let's begin with the consideration of practice in regard to food. So often when I talk about food I'm not just speaking about nutrition, but about breath, psychic food, or subtle food. But for now I will talk about diet. Our recommendation is for a lacto-vegetarian diet, with heavy emphasis on the use of raw, fresh foods, rather than lots of cooked pasta, boiled-to-death vegetables and casseroles. The particular chemistry of that raw-food diet most optimally serves our Work.

When animals are cultivated only to be eaten, the violence and brutality with which meat is treated, as it is being processed for market, is absorbed by the meat and transferred to the people who consume it. A wild stag, for instance, is a very different kind of meat than a deer raised in captivity. They are almost different animals, even though they are the same species and might look the same. There is no way of getting around the issue of "vibrations," i.e. of how things are influenced energy-wise.

Yet there are Native American and Eskimo cultures, and other tribal cultures, in which the way animals are killed and eaten is really a sacrament. So, ethically I'm not against killing animals in certain circumstances. But, energetically speaking, it takes three pounds of edible grain to generate one pound of edible meat in cattle, and that seems tremendously wasteful. I am dedicated, in principle, to the idea of conservation of energy or optimum use of resources. There is more life in raw foods, and a vegetarian diet is much more energy efficient than almost any kind of meat-eating diet in the Western world.

People need to train in an overall attitude of conservation of energy. This is very difficult given the standard of living we have in America, or in Germany, or other industrialized countries. The first time I went to India I noticed that what finally ends up as garbage there is totally unusable in any way, shape or form. A newspaper, for instance, after it's read, is then used to wrap food, and then used for insulation, and then used to cover up little beggars in the street. By the time newspaper becomes garbage it has basically crumbled into dust.

29

The women who travelled to India with me on that first trip were really buzzing about the fact that the Indians never used toilet paper. Instead, there was always a little, rusty pot of water available nearby, and you would just wash yourself and then dry off while you were walking down the road. Simple. For me it is not petty to suggest that people should use toilet-paper sparingly.

Our vegetarian diet supports conservation of energy, and because it relies on raw food, actually supplies the body with more nutrients, i.e., life energy. At the same time, when we travel and at celebration times on our Ashram we've been known to eat extraordinary amounts of sugar, meat, and highly refined or processed foods. In the times when we do eat meat, often it's to use a heavy diet purposely, either to ground something that needs to be grounded, or for other chemical reasons.

Sometimes, when food is prepared in an elegant and sophisticated way, another type of energy is added to the environment in which people are being together, and it is actually useful to eat that type of food. When we travel I will also make use of whatever food is typically eaten in the area we are visiting. Even though we might be "ugly Americans," perhaps by eating the local fare we experience being a little less ugly.

The first time we came to Germany I asked one of my German students if there was a Bavarian specialty, and among other things he described *schweinshaxen*. When we came back last year then, one of the first things we did was to find a nice place to eat and order *schweinshaxen* for everyone. And some of these people hadn't had a piece of meat in years, but they did okay with it anyway. Part of this is really indicative of the power of the laws of Divine Influence which are more significant than the power of the laws of digestion.

Students' willingness to trust their teacher is evidenced when they are ready to put the teacher's recommendations above their own idiosyncratic belief systems and morality. Obviously common sense is always involved, but this is an element that bears attention and recognition. A responsible student, moreover, is flexible and responsive to the need of the circumstances, not rigid and righteous because "raw vegetables are healthy and meat isn't and that's the way it is." If people go home to visit their families, they should eat what is served them. If your mother makes a big, beautiful, roast duck because that used to be your favorite food, don't say: "Oh, no thank you. I'll just have a piece of celery."

There's another important reason for cultivating flexibility. I heard a story more than sixteen years ago that impressed itself indelibly upon my mind. A woman was so horrified by reading the research about the effects of chemicals, preservatives and artificial coloring in food, that she completely revolutionized her diet. She began eating a very clean diet, specifically designed with all the proper nutrients. After being on this diet for years she went to a family party—a birthday celebration for one of her nieces—and they served cake with sugar and cream icing. Her family coaxed her to have it. "It's your niece's birthday," they said. "One little piece of cake won't hurt you." And despite her own resistance, she relented and had a piece of cake. She became violently sick.

There are two elements to consider here. First of all, most illness is psychosomatic. Since she was very neurotic she probably worked herself up into a state of fear, and therefore made herself sick. The other consideration is that the body does become so refined in its ability to absorb elements. In this case, this woman's body actually reacted to that piece of cake as if it were poison. On the other hand, certain cultures, like the Eskimos, might eat primarily one kind of food—like whale blubber (with occasional side dishes of whale liver, a little bit of whale tongue and every once in a while some whale testes). They simply wouldn't survive if they had to have what we define as a balanced diet with proper nutrients.

We need to be flexible because we never know what is going to happen. When Tibet was invaded by China, many of the Tibetans were captured and taken to re-education camps. There are some very dramatic stories of a few people who escaped from these camps. The things that they had to eat to survive, both in the camps and on the escape route, were seriously antagonistic to the dietary convictions they held before their capture. The body should not forget how to digest other forms of food besides just what is absolutely clean and perfect.

The question often arises about how to discriminate between the psychological craving for a type of food and the real need for that food in order to balance out something in the body. A lot of our work is to help eliminate the confusion we have between the messages we get from the body, and those that arise from the mind. There is no quick way to make that discrimination, but you can learn. The body knows, really.

The physical desire is just a matter of chemistry. It can be "positive" chemistry—something that the body needs that it hasn't gotten in a while; or it can be "negative" chemistry—an addiction, something the body needs in order to avoid crisis. But either way, it's a very direct and basic chemical process. There is no subtlety or subjectivity to it.

On the other hand, the mental desire for things (for particular foods, for instance) has to do with a totally subjective dynamic. For example, it's funny to watch people who think that they know the difference between fine wine and poor wine, when they really don't. They may know all the right movements—how to smell it, how to savor it on the tongue, or whatever—yet their response is often completely the effect of who in the room they admire and who they want to impress. It has nothing to do with what the wine tastes like.

Ego develops a particular strategy of relationship to life and to stimuli, and uses everything to reinforce the strategy: food, power, sex, everything. Our mental desire for certain foods is often a matter of how eating those foods will look to others. Sometimes we use food to substantiate something in ourselves that has nothing to do with the body, or with chemistry. Even the desire to be a vegetarian, for example, may be based on some very high ideal and yet may not be a reflection of sensitivity to what the body knows and needs. Maybe the mind just decided that vegetarianism was more ethical or moral.

The body knows. You need to keep your vision and remembrance of this kind of knowing, which we have all glimpsed at times. You keep using that as a reference. As you work with this you will discover that the genuine messages from the body will not be associated with a barrage of mental considerations. If you are providing what you need for yourself, very quietly and naturally, without any self-justification, you won't have to say to the people you live with, "You know, I'm going to have a hamburger now. Just relax. I'll explain it to you." Instead, there will just be no problem. NO PROBLEM. No crisis between what your body is telling you and your usual state of practice, or integrity, or your usual ideal.

I call the practices the Names of God because they were revelations. In many schools a vegetarian diet is recommended, meditation is recommended. So, some of the things we do are fairly common, and even some of the ways in which we describe them are not unique. At the same time, my particular purpose for offering these practices is because they were given to me to present as revelation, not because I saw them elsewhere and they made sense, and I figured, "Well, they're good enough for us too." Anything that is genuinely revelatory is not generated from one's own body of knowledge, even if it happens to be coincident to one's own body of knowledge. The ecstatic, mystical poetry of St. John of the Cross is an example of this. Some of this poetry is tremendously erotic, and "un-Christian-like," especially considering the time in which he was writing. He was highly persecuted for some of this writing because its implications were really antagonistic to traditional Church doctrine.

There are ninety-nine names of Allah and each name is a specific quality of God, like God the Compassionate, God the Merciful, and so on. Yet, in earlier times, many Sufis (the Islamic mystics) were killed for manifesting certain names of God if these were not within the legal definitions of the Koran. It is very important to me that spiritual "practices" not be used to take the place of genuine, spontaneous activity—praise and worship of God. If practices become like church dogma instead of a framework for one to work within which encourages the development of a refined and energetic response to life, then already they're not Names of God anymore. That's like repeating the Name of God in vain.

For any given spiritual master, the particular communications of that master are the Names of God, literally. Therefore, part of what generates the positive resonance between teacher and student is that the student, to the best of his or her ability, works in the specific way that the teacher recommends. If a Tibetan lama were your teacher, and that lama recommended a specific form of exercise or movement, a specific type of meditation, or a special diet, to follow those practices would elicit from the teacher what he had to offer. To give allegiance to a teacher and yet to do other practices, as if you knew better than the teacher, is one of the most extreme forms of arrogance.

On Meditation

The practice of meditation we use is very much like the Zen approach. We suggest that people just sit, for half-an-hour or forty-fiveminutes, or whatever is comfortable. There is no exact time limit, but it is advantageous to sit every day and at the same time of day if possible. During sitting you just observe what arises in your consciousness—that becomes the fruit of your meditation, the "food" you should work with for the rest of the day. So if you are feeling angry, as some of you have expressed, because in the meditation hall there is a picture of a male guru, then that is what you should think about, and work with, for that day. Ask yourself over and over: "Why does that make me so angry? What is really going on? What is the big deal. . .it's just some stupid guy, so what's the problem?" You use that to question yourself, " Who am I in relationship to my anger, my boredom, my resistance?" Like that.

Another way to work with what arises is to realize that your aim is not to erase egoic qualities, like pride, lust or greed, but rather to transform them. Every quality has two sides—transform pride and you have integrity. Lust transformed is passion. Greed transformed is charity or generosity. Therefore, as these raw elements of ego show themselves to you in meditation you "work with" them not by some yogic technique of transformation of energy, but simply by questioning, "What would this element be like if it were transformed?" or, "What is the upperworld equivalent of this underworld element?" You diligently inquire, of yourself. That's "working with."

Sometimes people say, "I had a bad meditation today," or, "I couldn't meditate today." They say that because what happened wasn't what they wanted to happen. They wanted ecstasy, bliss or visions and all they got was pain in the legs. Well, sometimes you will get visions, but not everyday. Sometimes the "vision" you get is of that picture in the meditation hall. Sometimes the feelings you get are very angry ones. That's just the way it is.

In the beginning, what usually arises is pain and boredom. The mind is like a monkey and it crazily jumps around to every kind of thought, every kind of resistance, interspersed with periods of creativity, clarity and bliss. But it is all mixed up. For most of us the first thing that meditation is about is, "...the pillow's too hard... the pillow's too soft...the window is open...it is cold...it's too warm...it's stuffy in here...." We might be meditating next to a bakery and for months our meditation is about what bread they're cooking. Then the phone rings or the dog barks next door and we are thinking about that, constantly obsessed with the details that hit us at the grossest level of our perception. The mind relies upon distracting our attention, fascinating our attention, and controlling our attention. The purpose of meditation is simply to observe what arises without a definition or an evaluation of that as being good, bad or neutral. You can't have a good meditation, or a bad meditation—whether your mind is confused and going quickly, or moving slowly with clarity, it's all meditation.

There was a Zen master in the last century or two, who would take a couple of shots of whiskey every night before bed. Many of his students thought he was just a drunk, but nobody had the nerve to ask him what he was doing. After many years someone finally got up the courage to pose the question. "Well," he said, "even after forty years of sitting my legs still hurt every time. So I take a couple of shots of whiskey because it relaxes me and takes the pain away so I can go to sleep easily." That's it. Often we look for secrets when what is happening is just very simple, very clear. No hidden meanings. It is the same with meditation, there are no hidden meanings. You just sit, and what arises is what there is, and no law says that you have to like it.

The process of meditation, as I teach it, is not in order to become relaxed and balanced. Simply to move through life with the idea that we're all children of God and we're all perfect the way we are, and we're all just evolving from lower forms of life to higher forms of life, is completely unacceptable. You see this approach in the "creativity" of most of the New Age, airy-fairy, head-in-the-clouds *artistes*. They paint those violet-toned, castle-in-the-clouds unicorns, with some woman in a sheer gown and long, floating hair, but they couldn't have a genuine relationship to save their lives, because they are still expecting to find the object of their fantasy. These are the guys who want to be relaxed and balanced, and their communication is certainly different from that of Gauguin, Bach, DaVinci, Michelangelo. That art was created not out of relaxation and balance, but out of turmoil, passion, and fire!

The point of meditation is to develop clarity of observation. Most of us never really stop to look at why we do what we do, why we think the way we think, why we emote the way we emote. To discover what the Work is, or what serving God is, and to know who we are, demands that we know why we do what we do and why we are the way we are. Most of the preferences that we firmly believe are intelligent, mature choices are no more than mechanical reactions to stimuli. As we gain clarity of observation through meditation, we may still have automatic responses to things, yet we will also be developing the discrimination to know if these automatic responses are interfering with serving God or not.

Seeing with clarity happens in moments, and in between those moments there's the same confusion, the same longings, the same desires. We need to be willing to deal with who we are in any given moment, and not assume that as soon as we hear the truth we're going to be perfect forever, and that's that. We *are* already enlightened, but to express that enlightenment every day in ordinary activity, is not our common practice. This is why on-going spiritual practice is necessary.

Sooner or later the mind will seek a deeper process, all by itself. Instead of gross physical distractions, it will then attempt to use more powerful and seductive means to fascinate us, distract us, or control us. If, however, we do not give it what it demands—if we do not indulge the fascination, the distraction, the demands to be controlled, but rather use the distractions as reminding factors, asking ourselves, "How can I relate to this?"—after a while the mind will go to the most powerful of its sources, to the point of inception, the literal source of its own arising.

If it could be said that we are looking for anything through meditation, that source-point would be it. When you reach that point of the literal arising of the mind you are on the borderline between two very distinct dynamics. On one side you find the dynamic of ego, the whole autonomous, mechanical definition that mind itself creates and sustains, and on the other side is the energy that we call the Will of God, that law of the continual evolutionary expression of all creation. If you just sit, eventually that's where your sitting will bring you, not because you design it that way, but because that's the way mind works. To reach that point is actually a function of the desperation of the mind, not a function of your successful meditation.

When one reaches that tangent point then there is a possibility of either going back on the side of ego, or falling onto the side of the Will of God. It's a very delicate moment. We've got a whole lifetime of habits that act as a magnet to pull us back to the side of ego. We're used to that side. We know the territory. It's comfortable. We've already learned all about it. The other side is unknown territory. The tendency is to have an experience of surrender to the Will of God, but then to flip back into our habitual patterns when the intensity of the experience begins to fade. Therefore, even when the process of meditation bears the fruit it's designed to bear we still need to continue to practice in order to build up a kind of sympathy with that fruit—a sympathy with the Will of God over and against ego. The language we use to express this is: "The body needs to literally construct a matrix that is capable of holding the kind of practice and work that comes with surrender to the Will of God."

Generally, everything about us, even our nervous systems, are submitted to the needs of ego rather than the needs of the Will of God. Surrender to that Will not only includes changing the mind and having a different disposition towards things, it also means completely restructuring the energy systems in the body. One can have the experience of surrender in a moment, but to begin to live that surrender requires time and hard work. That is practice.

On Exercise

Besides daily meditation and a vegetarian diet, we recommend regular, physical exercise. Occasionally I will give someone a specific type of exercise to do, but generally the exercise practice can be almost any form that people do on a regular basis, like walking, calisthenics, yoga. I most highly recommend traditional work like ballet or the martial arts. Depending upon the individual, Aikido or Judo or Tai Chi is usually preferable to Karate or Tai Kwon Do. I also like that Brazilian martial art called Capoeira. But I am not in favor of some brand new, experimental, "creative-movement" stuff that passes as exercise.

Study

There are other types of practice in this Work, but for now I will conclude with a brief treatment about study. Regular study is one of the recommended conditions for students in this school. Students study the books that I have written, as well as the world's traditional religious literature and also fine classical literature and poetry from both East and West.

Many people think they're supposed to study in order to build a great data-bank of "hints for the spiritually homeless" or something. Actually, to study properly is to allow what you're reading to contrast with your own personal experience. When you read something that "feels" true it will either resonate to what you already know or it will communicate that you haven't yet grasped this truth. Understanding is essentially irrelevant. If you read Sufi parables and you don't understand them, just read them anyway. There's no problem with not understanding something. Most of you probably know that sometimes you'll read something and it will make no sense at all at the time, but if you pick it up three years later it's very clear, even totally obvious.

Study, and other practices, are designed to help enable you to see things from many different angles, to get beyond a narrow viewpoint. To a four-year-old child, for instance, a doll may be as meaningful as the qualities of charity or gentleness may be to a sensitive adult. One of the common mistakes that adults make with children is that when a child's toy breaks the adult will say, "It's only a doll," because to the adult that's all it is. The adult recognizes that the child will get another doll, or could have a kitten or a dog instead. The adult knows that the child will come to love many, many things as she grows. Yet in the moment, our responses may be very insensitive. We adults are often not willing to view circumstances from the other person's perspective. That's one of the values of study.

When we went to India, we ate what the Indians ate, and travelled the way they travelled. We didn't rent a car, but rather went by public bus. At the same time, we did draw the line at just drinking the water everywhere. So, there is respecting another person's viewpoint or field of expertise, and there's also just plain stupidity. To be laid-up with dysentery for three weeks would allow us much less of any opportunity to appreciate the Indian culture. It is better to simply avoid drinking the water. The practices are also about developing good, common sense.

In Summary

The progression of consciousness is like this: First we are completely and neurotically identified with whatever arises. We think that this body is the only thing going on. We think that every element of our personality is just who we are, completely. Then we move into doing spiritual work. We move into a place in which we begin to observe our mechanicality from a higher position. We watch ourselves doing this and that and the other thing, and we're able to actually separate from what goes on—to objectively view what the body does, what the emotions do, etc. Finally, we come toa point at which we're neither identified nor disidentified with what arises. We simply draw no conclusions from anything. What arises is just what arises. There is no definition, no analytical process, no thought, and especially no problem about anything. "What is" is just "what is." That's where practice is moving us.

In Zen there's a saying: "When I first began, trees were trees and water was water and clouds were clouds. Then I was enlightened. I achieved *satori* after *satori* after *satori* and I found out that trees and clouds and water were so much more than I had ever imagined. But still I continued to work hard and to struggle for many years. At last the result of all my work was in coming to know that a tree is just a tree, and water is just water, and a cloud is just a cloud."

That's how it is.

Chapter Four

ENQUIRY AND THE DYNAMIC OF MIND

The source of our advantage as human beings, and also our problem, is what we call the mind. In this school we have a consideration which is summed up in the Zen-like phrase: Draw-no-conclusions-mind. The problem is not thought itself. Thought is the medium through which we interact with all the data which the senses absorb. The problem is that we interpret input-data subjectively, drawing conclusions about everything we experience.

There are three primary aspects of human consciousness: the mental aspect or thinking processes; the emotional aspect, which is the feeling process; and the moving aspect, i.e., our ambulatory functioning. Typically, data is first recognized by the mind even when it is felt with the body or emotions. We are feeling and moving beings, but our main form of interaction with the world is, by training, mental. If we were able to have Draw-no-conclusions-mind, input would be viewed with perfect objectivity so we would see things, and feel things, and move in relationship to things, directly, without any qualifications.

Let me give you an example. If you are in relationship with someone, and something about the way you are together generates pain, having Draw-no-conclusions-mind is simply to feel the pain, to know that it is pain, and to go on with the relationship. When we are functioning in the way the mind typically learns to function, however, we interpret all input subjectively—i.e., how it relates to us an object or subject. Instead of simply feeling pain and going on, we stop and say, "You did this to me." Or we say, "I'm no good," or, "I don't deserve this," or, "You don't love me." On and on and on endlessly. (And God forbid we should fall asleep, exhausted, before the other person is done blaming us for all their problems!)

The mind has a very strong investment in developing the illusion that it is the exclusive, controlling, manipulating factor in all circumstances of existence. That reminds me of a story about the mind.

A very upset woman went to a surgeon and said, "I have a snake in my belly and I need an operation." The surgeon talked to her delicately and eventually recommended that she see a psychiatrist. This insulted and angered the woman and she stormed out of the doctor's office and went to another surgeon with the same complaint. "I have a snake in my stomach," she said, "and I need your help to get it out." But this second doctor responded in the same way, telling her that she needed a psychiatrist.

As you can imagine, someone who has a snake in her stomach would find that to be a very disturbing thing and would want to have it taken care of, so she continued to go from doctor to doctor. Finally, she encountered a surgeon who had some experience with psychosomatic problems.

"So, you have a snake in your stomach," the surgeon said. "I can take care of it. Let's make an appointment."

The woman was so surprised. "You believe me?" she asked the doctor in amazement.

"Yes dear, of course," said the doctor, "I understand these things. We need to take the snake out so you'll be comfortable again." They made an appointment to have her in for minor surgery in a few weeks.

In the meantime, the surgeon went to a biological warehouse and bought a snake which was preserved in formaldehyde. When the woman came in for her appointment he put her under an anaesthetic, made a small incision, and then sewed it up so she would see that something had been done. When she woke up he showed her the snake, saying, "I had my doubts but you were so convinced, and now I see that you really did have a snake in you. I've taken it out and now you're fine."

The woman was very relieved. "Oh thank you," she said, "I feel wonderful, really great. But I would like to take the snake with me because none of my friends or family believed me and I want to show it to them."

So the surgeon gave her the snake and she took it home, stopping first to show it to her best friend who had been very critical of her.

"Look at this," she said delightedly to her friend. "You thought I was just crazy, and see, the surgeon took this out of me. I really had a snake in my belly."

The friend took one look at the snake and made a small gasp.

"What's wrong?" asked the woman, a bit disturbed at her friend's reaction.

"Well," said the other, "I hope he got it out before it laid eggs."

How the woman responded to *that* is left to your imagination.

Like I said, the body simply does what instinct requires, but the mind is tremendously manipulative. Even before birth, during pregnancy, the mind begins to develop a particular strategy that it will use essentially forever unless something alters that. And the strategy is always related directly to the mind's fear of extinction. For example, suppose that as an infant or young child you were left alone one night. Perhaps you cried until you fell asleep. Later when you awakened you had this primitive understanding that despite your fear and panic and confusion, you still existed. From that point on, the mind in its bizarre logic may begin to presume that survival demands that you be left alone, regularly. That's when people begin to set up their entire life-scheme with the mechanics and intention that they will always be left alone.

As adults, we develop intelligence, sensitivity, a full complement of feelings and responses to circumstances, and our logic becomes based more on common sense. We can readily *understand* the psychological dissonance that arises when we are left alone, yet we cannot stop *feeling* unwanted, unloved and greatly pained by it. We are relatively helpless to stop setting up the same situations again and again and again. These impressions made in infancy are unbelievably strong, and as we grow up and have more experiences, they are strongly reinforced. By the time we are mature adults we have this immense mountain of data to substantiate our neurotic strategies. It is like an upside-down mountain, however, because the entire mass of data rests primarily on those initial impressions received in infancy.

Most self-development processes begin at the top of this body of data and attempt to sort through it to the bottom, to that singular point where it all began. Yet even minimal intelligence should tell you that it is clearly impossible not only to make sense of that mass, but to begin to move through it in any direct way. Nonetheless we try. Many people wander for a lifetime amidst the tremendous labyrinth of what are really just the superficial and meaningless convulsions of the mind—the workings of ego, or the neuroses. Actually we have less chance of sorting through the mass of data that substantiates our survival strategy than we do of single-handedly digging Mt. Everest down to nothing.

There are two ways to come to some resolve about this problem of mind. The first method is this: If you can find the primal moment in which you developed a survival strategy, and if you can reanimate the exact intensity of consciousness that was operating at that moment, ostensibly you would have the possibility of bringing your adult intelligence and rational objectivity to that point and using it to choose a positive, and even ecstatic strategy, instead. Methods like primal therapy and rebirthing are designed with that principle in mind. Janov, the founder of Primal Therapy, claims that some practitioners of this method have actually grown several inches in height, and some women have developed breasts that were undeveloped before, as a result of this resolution. I have met people who have done these processes, and I have observed profound changes in their psychology, but I've never met anyone who has changed their primal survival strategy. To do that would be to experience the blessing side of the mind. And this, in itself, is viewed by mind as a threat to survival and autonomy. The mind will no sooner allow its ecstatic side to gain any ground than certain governments will allow freedom of expression, or freedom of the press. As soon as any underground currents of freedom, ecstasy, or blessing start to emerge, the mind, like the totalitarian government, tries to wipe it out—with torture, and occasionally with maiming or even death. It's very tricky, working with mind.

If the practitioners (therapists) of these primal, or psychological, processes do not have the objectivity with which to select a life-positive survival strategy, the client will reach that primal point and yet continue to exist with all the same neuroses intact. Without an already defined context of wisdom in relationship to the blessing side of the mind, just getting to that point and reanimating it leaves one confused and unsure of what to do. (Although most people claim they are very sure about what to do.)

A person who had truly shifted that survival strategy would not simply show more patience with his family. He or she would not just smile more, or no longer have a fear of heights, or a fear of water, or a fear of sex. Rather he would cease, altogether, to set up in his life the same kinds of survival programs or mechanisms that he had previously used.

The second possibility for dealing with the problem of mind is to simply sever the mind's relationship to conclusive or analytical thinking. The mind is like a computer that analyzes every bit of stimuli that is picked up by the senses. It then selects the stimuli that reinforce survival, and rejects what doesn't support it. If you sever the mind's analytical process, you have a senile and impotent dictator, just a figurehead with no power whatsoever. That alternative is the one that I would support. It's also the easier of the two.

This severing process is, by definition, Draw-no-conclusions-mind. It's clear, it's concise, it's exactly to the point. It could be qualified endlessly, but that's the definition. Have Draw-no-conclusions-mind, not as a practice (since it isn't something one *does*), but just as a state of consciousness.

Draw-no-conclusions-mind is enlightened life, and there are particular ways of practicing that will tend to attract that state. This enlightened state of "beingness" is not attracted from outside of oneself, but rather by eliminating those things that mask its presence in us already. The use of a rigorous form of self-observation known as "enquiry" is one way of attracting the state of Draw-no-conclusions-mind.

On Enquiry

The form of enquiry developed by the Indian sage, Ramana Maharshi, is to use the statement or the question, "Who am I?" as a constant form of self-interrogation. That particular phrase is also used commonly in certain forms of therapy where people sit with a partner and ask one another, "Who are you? Who are you? Who are you? Who are you? Who are you?" And whoever has the most patience wins!

We use another form of enquiry in this school, and it's not secret. It is written up in our books. Neither is it an initiatory *mantra*. Anyone can try it out, and some may actually feel that they are being successful with it. But, used out of the context of a direct relationship between student and teacher, it'll be no more useful than any other therapeutic technique. That is a very important consideration.

The phrase that we use for enquiry is, "Who am I kidding?" and it's important to use that fairly exactly because that particular phrase was revelatory. I didn't just think it up or start recommending it because I read that other teachers had used it. This practice was not created because it made rational sense.

The way to use enquiry is this: You have a problem, and you say to yourself, "Who am I kidding?" relative to that problem. What you may get is a feeling of detachment, or a feeling of fear, or whatever. Then you apply the phrase in relationship to *that* feeling. "Who am I kidding?" Whatever response you get then, you enquire about that, and you keep using the technique as a process. It is important that you not use it to get something in particular and then stop when you get something you don't like. If you use it with enough intensity, the results may not be comfortable at first. This question is like a *koan* in Zen. It acts as a burr under the saddle of ego. Enquiry is like providing a constant irritant, like a grain of sand in an oyster. Really, the beauty of a pearl is the result of an irritant, not the result of some artistic temperament on the part of the oyster. A lot of this work, unfortunately for us, has to do with the potential of the human being to create pearls as a result of constant irritation. So much of my job is to be an irritant. Naturally I would rather have the job of simply floating into the community of devotees and dispensing benediction, but other things must come first. Often I present irritation for a long time, and every once in a while in the middle of it all, a little gift of benediction shows up. Then everybody says "Ah..." and takes a breather, before getting back to the hard work again.

The use of enquiry is specifically designed to be addressed randomly to whatever arises in life, whether that is positive, negative or neutral. And it's probably more effective if it's not used during meditation but just throughout the day. After one becomes familiar with it, the question will arise by itself in very specific circumstances. You won't have to think about it. This spontaneous use is more effective than intentionally deciding when to apply it or not.

Enquiry works with the dynamic of ego, not with the expression of ego—which may be positive or negative, problematic or easeful. For the first few years in spiritual work, enquiry will be used primarily to reveal one's survival strategy.

It is so easy to fool ourselves. When people begin spiritual work they generally think, after a very short time, that their lives are transformed. Actually they bring to a spiritual community or spiritual practice the same dynamics that they previously brought to business or family life, but they don't realize that. If in ordinary life one was an aggressive, motivational speaker, when that one enters spiritual life where people are "supposed" to be silent and soft-spoken, that one may become the righteous flagbearer and expert on the *dharma*. That person's need to control, motivate and survive as she has always survived, has just put on a more attractive, "spiritual" face. Yet her context, and her basic reasons for acting, have not changed at all. So, to ask "Who am I kidding?" about everything is a valuable practice.

Some people are full of problems. Some people seem to have no problems. But we're all the same in one degree which is that we're all at the effect of ego. And in this relative world there's a vast ocean of experience that lies between ego and the Will of God. You need to practice enquiry for a long, long time before you really get a feeling for what it is. In the beginning, just using that phrase will generate a lot of different responses, but mostly on a superficial level. After some years, you will start hitting more and more refined levels. Enquiry will take you on a trip through that ocean of experience that lies between ego and the Will of God.

As you enquire you will uncover an entire underworld of phenomena. It can be terrifying. It's very important to have the attitude of moving *through* this underworld, observing the sights but not getting stuck in them, especially if you feel like you're being drowned or covered up. Enquiry itself does have some influence, some power. When used in the context of one's connection to a school and to the influence of the lineage of a teacher, it becomes a life raft in the ocean.

The phrase, "Who am I kidding?" refers to the essential nature of the Divine that is always being fooled by ego's strategies. If we try to articulate who the "who" is, the process will never work because it is only ego that can try to figure out who the "who" is. Enquiry is a form for ultimately bringing us to the root of the arising of consciousness, rather than for clarifying, rationally, our psychological dynamics. That will happen also, but it is secondary. Just because you get insights into your psychology doesn't mean that enquiry has worked. That's just a small part of it. Keep going, keep going, keep going. Keep pushing the technique as far as you want. The body knows how much it can handle. When you get a certain amount of input the body will demand some time to digest it. That's the way it is.

If life is lived always from the dynamic of duality, or object/subject consciousness, there is always a strategy of survival that is at work in every minute, even during sleep. Yet the truth is that the possibility of extinction of the being, or extinction of consciousness, is nonexistent. It's impossible not to survive! It follows that the part of us which is at the effect of our survival strategy is always being fooled.

Enquiry, as I recommend it, is a dualistic technique. It recognizes the paradox of duality—that although we are not separate, and in fact can never be separate, we still operate as if we are and still animate a survival strategy all the time. "Who am I kidding?" is a practical technique for use in the dualistic world—the world as we presume it to be, and therefore the "world" in which we need to work. As Jesus said, it's about "render(ing) unto Caesar the things that are Caesar's, and to God the things that are God's." (Luke 20:25) The context or texture of all our practice needs to be grounded in the practical realization of the paradox of incarnation. We are spirit alive in flesh.

Enquiry used properly, over years if necessary, will bring one directly to the primal source of the ego's survival strategy. Every single element of consciousness will be revealed to you. When you are finished observing all of it, the next step is simply to rest in *being*—a state in which there is no observation, no analysis, no revelation about anything whatsoever. That is the context of nonduality. That is Draw-no-conclusions-mind.

The possibility inherent in doing spiritual work is that we may sever the tendency to identify personally with every impression of mind that arises in us. It is possible to stop defining every impression that occurs as good or bad, and to stop trying to redo the "bad" ones, because really they never end. Even if you resolve the ones that you picked up in this life, if reincarnation is a fact you've got all the negative impressions of all your other lives to account for. It is very important to understand something: If there is only God, and if we are all actually connected to one another, then without some superhuman capability it would be impossible to tell whether the impressions that run through your mind are yours or anybody else's. And considering that there are four and a half billion people on the face of the earth, that's a lot of impressions. If we can't purify our own psychology, it's ridiculous to think about dealing with the psychological accumulations of vast cultures of which we know absolutely nothing. Psychological work has its value, but it's literally endless. Draw-no-conclusions-mind is still the best bet!

There is something called the "spiritual heart" which is the tangent point between our apparent separation and that domain in which there is no separation. There is a source of all thoughts, but there is no way to attribute those thoughts to any *thing* in particular. The point from which all thought arises is also the source of the entire universe, and reaching that point is the aim of a lot of spiritual practices.

The Body Knows

Another way of speaking about Draw-no-conclusions-mind is to say that "the body knows." "Knows what?" you ask. That question in itself already reflects a conclusion. "The body knows" means just what it says, without qualification. The body knows! The body knows, and at the same time the body rarely expresses its knowledge because mind enforces such a total control on all the elements of the being. If you pursue self-observation you may find that you're feeling "up" more of the time, and you very likely will consider this as some sort of linear progress. That may or may not be so. The mind wants to draw all sorts of conclusions from what it observes. If it were possible to simply be aware of changes of state without any analytical relationship to them, the body itself would answer your questions. Maybe not tomorrow or next week, but the body will answer your questions because your intention is to have your questions answered.

Actually there is only one answer for everybody in relationship to everything, but for most people that answer is simply unacceptable. Our inflexibilities, our conditionings, our education, our prejudices, our neuroses, all work to make it unacceptable. So the body has a hard time communicating through all of these barriers. Ordinarily the way the body expresses its knowledge is to give us a question of greater intensity than the question we may be considering at the time. Do you understand?

It is like in healing. Someone who has a serious illness may experience what is called a "healing crisis" which means that the illness gets worse immediately upon treatment, just before it starts to get better. It is the same when we speak about what and how the body knows. The body will magnify our question instead of relieving it, and some people view that as being a crisis, or being painful, or even wrong. But the optimal way to view that is as an opportunity. Even though temporarily it feels like the separation is magnified rather than integrated, integration is the natural result of this process. Eventually the mind will be integrated with the other ways of accessing. It will no longer be the controlling force. It will still make distinctions, but those distinctions will be meaningless, except as data. No distinction will be seen over and against other distinctions. There will be only unity.

But, there is no fast way for getting to that. I wish there was. I wish there was for you, and I wish there was even more for me.

Chapter Five

APPRENTICESHIP IN THE WORK:
WHAT IT TAKES TO JOIN THE CLUB

The definition of "being in the club" is serving God, which is, ostensibly, the highest principle in the universe. It is not surprising then that the desire to do this Work remains strong no matter what the obstacles.

This "club" is a very exclusive one, but not because the people in it are particularly extraordinary. It's exclusive because the degree to which one in the club is literally destroyed is not something that most people can manage effectively. You don't just join the club because you can afford the dues. The dues are whatever it costs you to get in.

Despite my warnings, and the witness of all the great traditions, and despite the sober looks on the faces of teachers who have grown old in this Work, everybody still thinks they really want to "be in the club." They must imagine that there is so much power here, or so much pleasure, that teachers just make these warnings to keep people away from the treasure.

Essentially, there is no way of earning or buying one's way into the club. It's sort of like a big hook falls from the sky and every once in a while it snatches somebody up and lands them into the club. There's no way of getting in by anything that you can do by yourself. The best that you can do is to stay as close to the club-house as possible, to optimize the possibility of getting hooked. If you get a chance to be a bus-boy in the club, or maybe a janitor, or a gardener, you grab it.

To participate in the Work is to be around it to whatever degree you can. And "being around it" doesn't necessarily mean physically close—like traveling to some physical place, some center. Rather, it means to hold a certain heartfulness, a feeling or mood. That heartfulness becomes a type of neon light, like the one the prostitute puts in the window to say she is available. Whatever the intelligence is that is the essence of what we call God sees the light in the window and reviews your resume, so to speak. Then, whenever somebody is needed for the Work, you get plucked! Plucked! Both like a chicken gets plucked and also like a fish gets pulled out of the water when it's hooked. And that's it.

So, now that I've told you there is nothing you can do to join the club, let me elaborate about how to stay around the clubhouse.

1. Initiate Yourself

Many people feel that to begin spiritual Work it's required that they have a formal initiation. I don't necessarily recognize this need. For me, formal initiations are not so much an entry *into* something as an acknowledgement of something. One gets out of this Work what one puts into it.

You get to be a student by saying that you want to be, and then we wait to see what happens. Certainly I will recommend practices, but you do with them whatever you want. Just go slowly, one step at a time, watching for feedback. Perhaps you will also write to me, and I may write back. I won't let you jump too quickly, even if you say you want to. You can try to jump, but I will not allow, or even encourage, over-indulgence. It is so common that in the heat of infatuation people want to give more than I think is necessary. But I won't take more than I think is reasonable from any one individual. So, already, a dynamic will be created between us. This type of interaction will quickly give you some idea of what it means to be a student of mine. Then you can decide whether that is what you really want or not.

There are a tremendous number of obstacles to really "joining the club." The reason for that is to discourage people from taking on something before they are strong enough to handle it. Otherwise they would be broken, and the Work is really not interested in just grinding people up.

I don't make the initiation. You make the initiation. You take a position, or stand, in relationship to your work, and that's the initiation. I am there to help you realize that stand; to confirm or deny it; to interact with it. But you make it! Every individual initiates themselves by virtue of what they're willing to give to the Work.

2. Engage Your Doubts And Questions

You approach the club by being willing to wrestle with questions about the things that bother you, or things that you perceive as inconsistencies. For instance, "You're just a man, like us, why are people bowing down before your picture?" The degree to which one realizes the value of this Work over and against some other form of Work, or Yoga, is the willingness they show for personally taking a stand, and then engaging their questions in an attempt to prove, or disprove, to themselves, that my claims to being a source of genuine help, my claims to offer something of the Divine, have some value.

Just start from wherever you are, take whatever opening you can find, whatever opportunity is given, and go from there. Move into this as gently as you want. Always begin slowly.

3. Develop Discrimination And Cultivate
   Your Hunger For Something Real

There was a Zen master, many years ago, who had only one teaching. No matter what question was asked of him, no matter what circumstances arose in which his instruction was called for, he would just raise his right hand, and point one finger straight up.

He was very popular and had a lot of followers who offered him many gifts and great sums of money and land and so on. It happened that one of his students observed all of this and decided that he'd like to share in the wealth. He said to himself, "Now that's a very simple teaching. Anyone could do it. Maybe I should go out and try for myself. I'll become rich and famous too, just like my teacher."

This student went to another country and he set himself up as a teacher. Every time someone would ask him something he would hold up one finger, just the way his master had done. Soon, many people began to gather around him and to become his students. He began to accumulate wealth—a big community, a huge temple, and so on. After many years he became quite self confident and arrogant, and decided that he should take a trip to visit his old teacher and show him how well he was doing. In his arrogance he imagined that they would be together as equals, have *dharma* discussions, and enjoy one another's enlightened company.

When he arrived at the home of the old teacher he was greeted graciously. "It is good to see you again after all these years," the master said. "How have you been and how have things been going?" The student, thinking himself to be highly refined and sophisticated, smiled at his teacher, then slowly raised his hand and pointed one finger straight up. At that, the teacher pulled out a knife and without hesitation cut the student's finger completely off.

Blood spurted everywhere. The student started running around the room, screaming hysterically, "Oh my God, are you crazy? Are you insane? You cut off my finger. What am I going to do?" But the master simply smiled at him, raised his hand in the familiar gesture, and pointed one finger. Well, as the story goes, in that instant the student realized perfect enlightenment—which was his aim all along. And they all lived happily ever after.

As with all stories, there are many levels on which it could be interpreted, and many considerations that can be made about it. Let me make a few.

First of all, there is a saying that "the best form of praise is imitation," which is the basis for all the style changes in clothing, for designer jeans and sunglasses, and so on. But the thing about imitation, which also is probably as true in the spiritual domain as it is in the supermarket, is that you get what you pay for. Because something looks like something else doesn't mean it serves the same function. It can, but it might not. For instance, there was an old television show called "Candid Camera" that used to be very popular. For purposes of entertainment, ordinary events would be changed in some strange way and then innocent people would interact with these circumstances, not knowing that they were being recorded on film. In one case they took the engine out of a car, and then with some hidden source of electrical power had the car drive into a gas station. The driver would then ask the attendant (whose reactions were being filmed) to check the oil. The gas station attendant would open the hood of the car and be utterly dumbfounded. There was no engine in it—a car that he had seen, with his own eyes, just minutes ago, drive into the station!

Even though that car looked exactly like a car with an engine, you couldn't say that it was the same. To know the difference, however, you'd have to look inside. Often the difference between a school, or structure, in which there is Real Work available and a school in which there is merely a lot of inventiveness and quick thinking, is not apparent on the surface. One has to look "under the hood" to experience the actual essence that may be present. There aren't a lot of people who are willing to do that.

In the example of the student who got his finger cut off, just on the surface it looked like extreme violence on his master's part. But, that act of violence was the means by which the student realized enlightenment. Once he got it, moreover, he was then able to go back to his own students and authentically represent the teaching he had assumed he was presenting before. Now, everything would be different, even though things might look exactly the same. (And, since "people are people" everywhere, probably most of his students, sensing that something was different, would leave him immediately, cursing him for it. They would set out again under the guise of looking for a "real teacher," someone who was enlightened according to their definition.)

The second point of this story is that changes in form are often provocative in a way that shifts people's ordinary expectations into a whole different domain. When Meher Baba was a young man he went to a woman teacher who kissed him on the forehead. That teacher's act catapulted him into six or seven months of completely non-dual ecstasy. Then he went to another teacher who threw a stone which hit him right where the woman teacher had kissed him. That began the process of integration of the non-functional ecstasy into a functional teaching capacity. Shock can be a most vital catalyst for change.

If I were going around teaching about how to channel the Ascended Masters, probably lots more people would be attracted, and we'd make lots more money. Imagine how interesting and exciting that would be! The air would be abuzz with the intensity of people's enthusiasm. I'm not interested in those kinds of effects, not that I ever mind enthusiasm (as long as what is being touched is "being," not just fascination with phenomena).

Anyone who wants to "join this club" needs to have a genuine hunger, not just a need to be simply distracted and comfortable.

4. Consider the Nature of Apprenticeship

To approach this club is much like entering an apprenticeship program with a master. When a master of any craft accepts an apprentice, he or she only accepts one who has demonstrated some physical ability to master the craft. The next step is to find out, through labor and testing, whether that person also has discipline, integrity and consistency. It is the same in entering this Work. No one is accepted as a student who doesn't have the possibility for equality with the master. But, beyond that, the more immediate question is, can you bring here what this Work requires—namely tenacity, sacrifice, surrender, and genuine tensile strength? This Work, as it progresses, will demand as much of you as you expect of it.

A man who studied Aikido in Japan told me a story about his friend who was the highest-ranking Westerner in the practice of *Kudo*, which is archery. The story concerns the time that this practitioner was to be tested for his third rank in *Kudo*. To appreciate the story you must understand that the context of practice in the Orient is very different from what it is in the West. Students are not expected to ask to be tested unless they are sure they can pass the test. To fail is to insult one's respect for the teacher. To fail is to imply not that the student is a bad student, but rather that the teacher is a bad teacher. Respect for one's teacher is a very highly demanded element of one's relationship to training in any kind of apprenticeship program.

The test for this *Kudo* rank required one to shoot three arrows, very fast, one after another, and to hit the same mark, exactly, every time. Now this Western student had practiced hard, especially because this was his second attempt at this test. The first time he had hit the target twice, but had missed with the third arrow. In the second test, however, he was successful. All three arrows landed right on target, perfectly. With a sigh of relief the student relaxed his tension and looked to the master, expecting to see a smile of approval. The Master just looked annoyed, and shook his head "no."

The student was shocked at first, and then a bit angry. Not only did he not understand why he didn't pass, but he also felt remorse at having shown disrespect for his teacher. He was angry both at the teacher, and at himself. So, he asked the master, "What have I done wrong?"

"You finished your third shot," said the teacher, "and then came back into position, but your bow was not close enough to the ground. You were six inches too far from the ground."

"You never told me that," the student argued. "You never explained that."

Looking very annoyed and very impatient, the teacher said: "Well, I can't tell you everything. You're supposed to pay attention."

The man recognized this to be true, and so passed the test on the next try.

It is much the same here in this club, in this apprenticeship. Most of the elements of this work you get by paying attention, not by being specifically instructed.

5. Be Available To Receive Help

Believe it or not, being available to receive help was as difficult for me to recognize as it might be for some of you. There are individuals who provide a direct form of help in my life. We are equals, and yet I realize that their experience in this Work is more encompassing than my own. I am very grateful for this now because it spreads out the responsibility, but in the beginning I wasn't so appreciative. I thought I was such a great teacher, and that I knew everything, and I...I...I.... "I'm not going to take help from anybody else." But then it became necessary. It is necessary to everyone to be helped. When you join the club you will stand alone, but to stand alone is not to be out of relationship, particularly relationship to help.

It should be obvious by the experience of Christianity, Islam, Hinduism, that without an active guiding force personally present in people's lives, that the possibility for misinterpretation of the original teachings is almost endless. It is my observation that if a teaching is not embodied in a living representative, it's so open to misinterpretation that it is almost impossible to really know what the original teacher was attempting to communicate.

I am represented as a guru, and this may be both presumptuous and arrogant, and may certainly generate some resistance on the part of many individuals. But, through my own experiences, I have realized that recognizing the help of a living individual is of such greater significance than what can be provided by scripture, or by the histories of people who are no longer around. I feel in complete integrity, therefore, in continuing this process. I set myself up this way, and I allow my students to continue to reinforce that structure. And you must know that I do so not with a sense of delight and appreciation, but more with a real sense of hesitancy and stark recognition of the possible pitfalls and dangers of that.

I realize that the circumstances certainly encourage a hierarchy—and that some people feel a relationship of inferior to superior. But that's okay with me too. Bluntly speaking, I have paid my dues, and you haven't. I'm the teacher. I make the rules. I wrote the books. I work the space. And if you have a problem with that, it's just too bad.

In tribal societies in which the dynamics of ego are not as bizarrely defined as they are in the Western world, the differentials in job function in the tribe are communally recognized, tacitly. It is just obvious to everybody who is best equipped for doing what. There's just no problem with it. Considerations like those of equality, of a guru-student relationship, of superior and inferior, can only be resolved through the transformation of the ego structure, not through verbal qualification. And that's hard work.

I am very critical of those who will not take a living teacher because of the necessary struggle involved. How can we work on ego if ego itself is defining what the elements of the work are in the first place! It's impossible. It is popular today for people to say, "We are our own best teacher. Everything we need is within ourselves." I would agree, and disagree.

Every false culture is based upon an instinctual recognition of what is true. But, the way that recognition manifests itself is through the filters of the survival strategy. Thus, the statement that our real teacher is inside, and that we have everything we need but only need to access it, is an instinctual recognition of the philosophical truth that there is only God. One who says this, however, lives inside a bubble of isolation. By his or her own definition, no help is possible to this being. The filter through which this typically

"New Age" idealogy has been generated is often this: "If I acknowledge that I am already that which I seek, and I believe that deeply enough, that will be an absolute protection against ever having to be vulnerable, in a real way, to anyone else or any form of help."

Time being the great help that it is, however, and given the right circumstances, people with any degree of self-honesty will come to realize, if not admit, that the inner teacher isn't working. "It" may give them fast answers, or even correct fast answers, but it doesn't transform egoic suffering into compassion. That is what I have to offer. To "join the club" means a willingness to use me as teacher. It means that you will stay around long enough to get a sense of what is really going on, and I won't make that easy. I could act very soft, and feminine, and receptive, and nurturing, and empathic, but that wouldn't affect what I'm looking to affect. I am looking to provoke individuals to move through the obvious veils that are put up. I want them to diligently search out what's behind the veils.

There is something behind these veils. I believe it is something of significance, and something which is free of ordinary human biases and prejudices. As you get to know me, it will be up to you to decide whether or not that is true.

There are a sequence of realizations that people have in relationship to my teaching work. The first tends to be a very strong response to the feeling of patriarchy. (I design it that way on purpose.) The second level of realization, which sometimes takes quite a bit of time, is that I actually represent the feminine, not the masculine. Beyond that, long beyond that, is the realization that my value as a teacher has to do with one's possibility of entering through this doorway into the completely non-dual reality. But, to enter the doorway of nonduality one must first pass through the initiations of masculine and feminine polarities.

My intention in presenting a very defined patriarchal energy in the beginning is because I want students who won't easily become "followers." I don't want an army of women ready to die for the cause! (And that idea may offend you because you might think that would never happen to you. What I've found is that liberated women, feminists, when they "fall" for a cause, even a cause as seemingly antithetical as the company of a male teacher, they become militant! You couldn't budge them with an atom bomb, because actually the whole feminist movement is not so much a movement into femininity as it is a reaction against masculine dominance.)

6. Refuse To Be A Follower

A follower is somebody who likes the ideas connected to a spiritual school or a spiritual teacher, and is willing to do anything for the idea, but has no resonance in the body. Followers, therefore, are very dangerous people because they have no sense at all of the repercussions of interactive energy dynamics. They are like lemmings, willing to go off the cliff for no reason, without any thought, just because they like an idea. They will die for the cause and hence have a strong tendency to become fanatics.

In America I have seen bumper stickers on cars which say, "The Bible said it, I believe it, and that's it!" (Probably the inspiration of some fundamentalist Christians.) To me that indicates a very dangerous personality dynamic which can be observed in many types of spiritual work. There is a fine line to walk in this regard. In the beginning of one's work with me, if I were not to allow some elements of infatuation or tendencies toward exaggeration, I would have almost no students at all. Maybe none. At the same time, I'm well aware of how this dynamic operates, and I dislike it. Over time, I make it clear to people when they are functioning from this follower mentality with me, and I make it known that they need to shift their disposition. Gurdjieff, whose teaching work I admire quite a bit, was someone who was extremely harsh on this follower mentality, and, as a result, during his life he had a very small but strong following. The closer one gets to the heart of the Work, the less leeway one has for those kinds of flirtations.

One gets close to the heart of the Work not by being physically close to me, but by being something in their own presence, in their own Work.

A student, as distinguished from a follower, is someone who is willing to participate in the Work the way the teacher defines it. He or she doesn't necessarily have all the answers, or even a complete trust in the teacher. A student feels some value and wants to find what that value is in his own life. Over time, then, greater trust develops, greater respect for the teacher, greater willingness to participate.

Beyond follower, beyond student, there is the devotee—one who has realized that the teacher is the doorway to God. This one is willing to do whatever is necessary to move through that doorway. Such a one might still have a tremendous amount of conflict with the form or style of the teacher's work, even with the environment in which the teacher lived, yet this one could still be a devotee.

The woman who translated *Beelzebub's Tales* (one of Gurdjieff's main works) lived with Gurdjieff in France when she was quite young. She was only in her twenties, and quite beautiful. She continually heard stories of Gurdjieff's immoral lifestyle, how he was always hopping into bed with most of the women that he met. Yet with her that was not the case. Gurdjieff was extremely respectful, elegant, and sensitive, so she found these stories hard to believe.

One day she asked Gurdjieff about these rumors. "Were they true? What did they mean?" His response to her will be long remembered.

"All my sins are on the surface," Gurdjieff said, and then went on to explain that the essence and integrity of his teaching Work was really untouched by his apparent behavior. For many students, it was too much to handle. They left him. Those who were able to see beyond the behavior found something priceless, something which at the time was unavailable any place else.

A devotee recognizes the Work, above all, and the teacher is seen simply as a conduit for that Work. The devotee will do whatever is necessary to integrate that Work into his or her own life.

There are no universal doorways to the Work, only human doorways. One is called *devotee* because he or she has a devotional relationship to another human being as gateway to God. (No, the clouds are not a gateway to God... I'm sorry to tell you. Neither is the Black Forest, as wondrous as it is. It's not a gateway to God.) Obviously a lot of so-called teachers, who are not gateways themselves, still refer to their students as devotees. Genuine teachers are not that common. So, whether I, in fact, am such a gateway is something that each of you will have to discern for yourself. And that will take some time, and some attention.

If I am not your teacher our time together can still be very useful to you. Any real teacher makes a communication that can be used by any other real teacher. What we do together will be available to you when you find *your* teacher. But, one way or another, you do need a teacher. Ego is so sophisticated that it can excuse itself in so many ways from the need for real help. We need an objective guiding factor to keep us on track. Most of us are self-deluding enough to go right up to the moment of death thinking that we have really got it covered. But, then it is going to be too late. You need to start now. This work doesn't wait for anybody. If you don't enter the Work, it will just roll right over you like a steam roller.

7. Use What The Master Has To Offer

Life, to me, is not worth preserving at any cost. Simply being ambulatory isn't life. If my life is not sustained by a very refined quality of "food" I'd just as soon be dead. It really doesn't make any difference to me. My relationship to my students, to my family, to my mother (who is still very much alive), has got to be more than just the fact that my presence "brings something" to those in my environment. If they are not receptive to that presence and willing to really engage it, then to hell with them. They can do without me. I am not interested in people "needing" me. Let them go out and need somebody else. Needing someone is a pretty easy thing to do. A master is only interested in being used.

Three things are required for people to make use of what a master might be able to offer. The first is intention. You have to want to make use of it. Since most people are fairly sincere when they approach this Work, that is almost a given. The second thing is discipline, or will, or attention. Any of these words can be used in the same way. Just because an individual thinks they're some great spiritual hero, doesn't mean anything. You have to have the ability to actually *do* something with what you get. That becomes more difficult because for many people, as much as they might desire to work, they are too weak to follow through.

The third quality is to have the physical capacity to handle what one gets when one works. If one does a little bit of spiritual work and starts "blowing fuses"—emotional and physical fuses; or if the nervous system starts misfiring and then shorts out, that is not particularly useful to the Process.

The more these three qualities are present in any given individual and the more I recognize their ability to feel the real meaning of this Work, the less information I give them. Then, they simply get an opportunity dumped into their laps. They either make use of it or not, but I offer no explanations.

It is important to realize, however, that my ability to give people precisely what they need for their spiritual work is not a matter of either psychological observation on my part or an educated guess. It's a matter of pure instinct. There is no intellectual preparation on my part for what goes on between me and any individual or group when I am working with them.

The value of a teacher is not in the teacher's expertise at analyzing people's types and dispositions, or "playing with the engine," so to speak. If a teacher is not submitted to something more, to what I call, Divine Influence, (and every teacher has his or her own words for it), if a teacher does not carry or convey a Presence that is transcendent, there is no value whatever in his simply poking people's irritation buttons.

8. Develop a Feeling-Sense of Resonance with Divine Influence

The domain of dualistic processing and the domain of no-separation (of already present union) are as isolated from one another as night and day. There is a resolution between these two domains that integrates them until ultimately there is no paradox or conflict between duality and nonduality. That integral chemistry or dynamic is called, in my language, Divine Influence.

Divine Influence cannot leap the chasm between the Divine domain and the ordinary domain. A bridge is needed. The Spiritual Master is that—literally the bridge between the Divine domain and the ordinary domain.

Many people ask if that bridge has to be a human being, or could it just be the forces of nature, or something. I hold that it must be a human being; human beings need "something" (someone) with a chemistry similar to their own in order to bring them into alignment. Paradoxically, the teacher is neither completely human nor completely Divine, but has one foot in either domain. Somewhere on that bridge is the way for others to pass.

To the untrained eye it looks as if the teacher simply collects students as a kind of self-aggrandizement. It's understandable that it would appear that way. In actuality, the Spiritual Master is that through which a person's consciousness needs to pass, and a chamber in which resolution between the dualistic and the non-dualistic domain occurs.

When you study with a teacher, any teacher, it's crucial that you *feel* the teacher's intention more strongly than you use the teacher's lifestyle as justification for either studying or not studying with him or her. Historically, there are many examples of profoundly effective spiritual masters whose lifestyles were apparently anything but spiritual, or moral, or consistent. Gurdjieff, whom I mentioned earlier, was one. There are great teachers who were drunkards, drug addicts, sexual libertines, liars and thieves. Some were even violent. It doesn't make any difference.

Often, the elements of what some teachers will call compassion might seem to be actually cruel, but then you need to align yourself to the feeling of what the teacher is doing before you can make a value judgement on the form of the manifestation. Information is useful, but what is more useful is an instinctual feeling of what this Work is, and the willingness to be responsible, whether you understand it or not. "Mere understanding," as Werner Erhard has said, "is the booby prize."

For most people, to lose is to win. What I mean by that is, for the ego to lose in relationship to God is to win in relationship to itself. To intellectualize is to define your life based on the manipulations of the rational mind rather than to allow your life to be defined by the mood of the body. When you move into this Work your mind won't stop, but it will cease to control you the way it does now. So there you have it.

Now that you know all that stuff about how hard this Work is, and how most people don't know what they're getting into, and all that shit...just watch your step. Don't look a gift horse in the mouth, which means, don't run away from opportunity, but don't jump in over your head. That's all. I still like to think that I don't let people jump in over their heads (which is probably quite presumptuous). I think some of my students might disagree, however, particularly those who are going down for the second time and haven't learned to swim yet.

Chapter Six

ON WOMEN AND MEN:
TANTRA, SEX, RELATIONSHIP AND LOVE

Philosophically, there is nothing that exists that is not God. That's fine and it's true. But practically, when human beings need to earn a living, find comfort, relate to one another and appreciate elegance, art, and so on, philosophic truisms are meaningless. My particular form of teaching has to do, first, with considering the obstacles that keep us from realizing the Divine, not with speaking a lot of sweet and inspiring poetry about God that doesn't make a difference in people's lives. I am very practical, grounded, and direct in terms of what we need.

The nature of the Divine is dualistic in the sense that all manifestation is made up of attracting opposites. Energetically, then, men and women are like positive and negative electrical poles, or like the north and south polarites of a magnet. Essentially, men and women should attract one another. If that is not happening...if men don't solve this *koan* of women and women don't solve the *koan* of men, then we can forget about understanding the nature of God.

The sexual revolution has hit the Western world like a storm and yet people are more unhappy in sexual relationships than ever before. Now, even though people can have every kind of electrical contraption, and all sorts of books and movies about "how to do it," people are "doing it" worse than ever before.

Why are we so enraptured by sex? Simply because of how it feels? No. We are enraptured by sex because we die somewhere in it. We die in sex, and that's what we're looking for. We are desparately looking for something to make us forget this disruptive world we live in, and sex is supposed to make us forget. We keep using it more and more to that end. But, it doesn't really work. The second after a fifteen or twenty second orgasm, it's done, and you remember your suffering again. We want to die desperately, to end our suffering. We want to be born again, desperately—to feel! We want to wake up, desperately. That's the big attraction to sex.

What you will find as you seriously apply yourselves to spiritual Work is that you will tend to outgrow sex in the terms that you see sex as now—as a release, as pleasure, as a high point in the day, as the way you manipulate or are manipulated. Sex will tend to take its place in your life along with everything else as a natural and spontaneous response to the moment, in the instinctually appropriate time and place, mood and attitude.

When sex is seen for what it really is, which is communion with the Goddess or communion with God (depending upon whether you're man or woman), then the pleasure you derive from sex becomes grounded in Reality. There is much more involved in "communion with the Beloved" than simply the act of intercourse and orgasm. There is so much more. Even when the act is accompanied by emotional feelings of pleasure, happiness, attention…there's still more. But, you can't get on to more until you've been grounded in Reality, i.e., you have to be doing just what you're doing.

In my opinion, the Divine is not discovered by becoming more and more "far out." The Divine is discovered by becoming optimally normal.

✛ ✛ ✛

Recently I was looking through a popular German magazine all about tantra workshops and "finding bliss through tantra…" And I thought that the whole issue was one of the worst excuses for self-masturbatory indulgence I had ever seen. In these workshops people get to look at other people naked, and then to pat themselves on the back and say, "Aren't I great? Aren't I good at sex?…and free?…and wonderful?" I'm telling you it's all shit!

In one book I read the author recommends that for one month the partners are not supposed to touch. So they start out, the first week, sitting across the room from one another, clothed, and they just look at each other (ya know, the old, misty-eyed romantic bit). The second week they sit directly in front of one another, clothed, and they look in their partner's eyes for an hour, (probably hiding lust behind "the gaze" of course.) The third week they take their clothes off and sit and look again. And the fourth week they sit without clothes on, and with knees touching. Then one is supposed to be primed for real tantra. Can you imagine that these books actually tell you to do that?

Well, by the time the four weeks is up, people jump on one another like they're mad, and what takes place then is eighty percent fantasy, and twenty percent physical. Of course they have a great time! Who wouldn't after a month of percolating repressed passion? Of course the experience is going to be overwhelmingly powerful. But it's fantasy. It's not tantra.

Another approach some authors take to "tantra" is to show you all these amazing positions—upside down, backwards, from the front, from the back, or with fingers, toes or noses…. Here again, real tantra doesn't have anything to do with what position you're in. It makes no difference at all.

Conventional sex is a matter of self-satisfaction. If you look at the media, and at advertising, sex is blatantly used as a commodity, and any faint tendency towards Real sex is completely overridden by the neurotic need to copulate in a fashion consistent with

71

the media hype that's been fed to us all our lives. We're supposed to do it like a playboy, or a playgirl, like a "swinger" or a "stud"! The biggest offenders are the high-class "ladies" magazines. The articles in these magazines encourage the most unrealistic and superficial sex and relational activity that one can imagine. They may not be pornographic, or particularly explicit, but they encourage women to be sappy, sentimental, bitchy and adolescent.

In the same way in men's magazines, men are encouraged to be tough when they need to be, understanding and tender when they need to be, and to know everything there is to know about women, sex, travel, cars, money and food.

Most of what is associated with sex today is simply a neurotic tendency to do and be who we've been trained to think we *should* be as men and women. There's so little real enjoyment in all of this. People are doing lots of things to get their bodies to feel good, but we know that's not enough. A short time after a massage, when the body, or the mind, starts to feel less good again, we start looking around for another "hit." Without some understanding, some tenderness, warmth, a relationship. . .it doesn't matter how good the body feels. The things that really feel the best don't have to do with the parts of the body that are touched. They have to do with the attitude that is brought to bear in the relationship. If the man can be a Man to a woman, that feels infinitely better than what he does to her body.

Men will always be a mystery to women and women will always be a mystery to men. Becoming great sexual technicians is the fastest way to destroy the mystery. Yet to a frustrated and dissatisfied man or woman, a partner who is a good technician seems like a really successful partner, but that is a veneer that fades very quickly. Likewise, if one simply wants to be fairly proficient at life, and completely and unavoidably separate from God, then one should look to become a good technician; but no degree of technical proficiency will effect communion with God.

Of course, a good technician is quite capable of igniting a few nerve endings in the brain, and that might *look* like God, or even *feel* like God. But any kind of experience, no matter how ecstatic, that does not transform the experiencer into someone who essentially knows how to be with children, how to be with their family members, how to be with their mates, how to be with all of life, is not God! Natural and ordinary life, the way it is, is the alchemical crucible—the space in which transformation happens.

The Divine is not meant to be discovered in heaven. If that were the case, we would *be* in heaven, not here. And, despite the philosophy that the kingdom of heaven is "here and now," and that we have to make our lives here heaven. . . I'm sorry to have to tell you that this ain't heaven!

The Alchemy of Transformation

Since ancient times it has been known that the sexual act is literally a generator, and a catalyst. Many spiritual masters and adepts have used sex as a method to encourage communion with higher levels of consciousness. In a sense, they were evolving the human race through the use of sex. It's very common to see pictures from ancient China, and from the Hindu and Buddhist traditions, showing the gods with their consorts. In the Orient, beautiful artwork was designed to celebrate sexual union in its transcendent capacity. People weren't embarassed about it.

The communication in real tantra has to do with the understanding of the woman's energy and the man's energy. True tantra is founded in the already present knowledge that you are not separate to begin with. True tantra has to do with a crystal clear understanding of man, woman, and alchemy.

Women might be described as basically being receptive, and men as basically being aggressive. Since women symbolize *Shakti*, the Goddess, form, activity, movement, energy, and men symbolize *Shiva*, who is the formless Absolute, who is simply consciousness—the union of *Shiva-Shakti* involves *ascent* by the woman, and *descent* by the man. When *Shiva* and *Shakti* become one another, that's what is called perfect union. Then the sexes disappear and there is only what is arising in the field of Reality. When this process is happening for a couple, orgasm can happen, but non-localized, non-ejaculatory orgasm (by the man) keeps his energy connected to the woman and doesn't rip him away from her.

The physical practice of tantra by men involves the utilization, but not necessarily the strict preservation, of semen, in conjunction with the proper disposition of sexual energy and *intention*. The subtle practice of tantra involves the right use of *attention*. The same principle applies to women, of course.

When sexual activity is somewhat regular, a lot of semen is produced in the man, and a lot of sexual fluid in the woman. When this fluid is allowed to be reabsorbed into the body, rather than expelled or expressed, the chemistry involved in that fluid is sympathetic to certain hormonal secretions by areas of the brain—like the pineal gland, which is traditionally associated with the "third eye." We don't know all that these glands can do, but we do have a high degree of circumstantial evidence that stimulation of these glands can produce mystical vision, revelation, higher creativity, and so on. The utilization of sex is one way of activating the higher glands.

I recently read a book of love letters written by the composer Chopin, who was a creative genius in the realm of art, and probably could have been a saint if he had chosen to. In these letters he expressed his passion to his lover. But, he said, "When I'm with you and we're screwing all the time, I can't write . . . not even a line of music. And being away from you here. . ."(he was on vacation), "I've been writing like a champ." (I'm modernizing his language.)

Without knowing its full impact, many people have stumbled upon a connection between expending life energy through ejaculatory orgasm and retaining that life energy—though not necessarily through the avoidance of sex. These people have realized the dynamic and energetic "edge" that can be created by using sex in this way. They have learned that the daily tensions can actually be transformed into a source of phenomenal fuel. Now that's alchemy!

The psychological adjustments necessary to beginning a practice of physical tantra are perfect opportunities for work on self. All the "crap" you've been hiding for years, relative to your sexuality, will start to surface. There is some deep, primal stuff surrounding ejaculatory orgasm. It's a relatively easy process to avoid orgasm physiologically when compared to the challenge of the emotional and psychological effects. And it is hardest for men. Women have a much easier time learning to resensitize their bodies. Men think they need that genital ejaculation to feel like real men. The idea of full-body orgasm is completely foreign to most of them.

You should go into sex high, and come out higher. Not go into it low and come out relieved! The former is regenerative sex. The other is degenerative. Regenerative sexuality, however, is of no value if everything else that you do is degenerative. You can appreciate this in another area—the use of dietary supplements, which I think are great. But if you drink, and smoke and eat "poisons" or junk foods, then you can't expect the dietary supplements to clear out your body. Some people do this with sex. They try using tantra while the rest of their lives are degenerative. Nothing of any value will ever happen that way.

Sexuality should not be used as another hold on someone, as a tool or as a bargaining point. That's grossly immature. Sexuality should be expressed in relationship between two people as the fullness of their lives together in God, not as another "noose." It might be "winning" in one respect, but it is actually using what should be prayer to the Goddess, both for men and women, for petty and egoistic purposes.

Life itself should be regenerative. Bodily, emotionally, physically, energetically, you should be singing the praises of God all the time. You should be chanting, enjoying life, being happy with people, exercising, eating the appropriate foods. Then sex can be both generative and regenerative, actually. Sexuality should always be a matter of fullness between individuals.

In tantra work you can't relax. You've got to keep your eyes open and pay attention. The traditional practice of tantra essentially means meeting and going through the elements of the underworld, rather than attempting to escape them, as a way to realization. We need fears, desires, illnesses, greed, possessiveness, and all of the life-negative qualities that each of us has to some degree, and through working with them we transform them.

Passion is wonderful, and to bypass ordinary, natural passions is to fail to be a man or a woman and to fail to understand incarnation on Earth. The attempt to bypass ordinary passions is also the psychological response of being terrified of the kind of vulnerability that sex demands. Subconsciously one may decide, "This stuff is just too heavy for me. I'd better pretend that I'm some pure, angelic mystic and be celibate!" Sex provides a kind of vulnerability that is not found elsewhere. (Probably the closest thing to it might be what is shared by the survivors of a plane crash, or some other profound event in which great hardships are experienced together.) Not even in the deepest friendships do you get that kind of chemical vulnerability. Your body changes when there is real chemical sympathy with other people, and most people can't share that kind of vulnerability with more than one person and not be torn apart by it internally. We're not wired that way. (Although you can learn to alter the wiring, but that takes instruction which is not commonly available. You don't get that in these popular tantric workshops. You get that by a lifetime apprenticeship.)

Different tantric schools use different elements in their practice—sex, or alcohol, or tobacco, or other things. Yet they are all the same in their focus on the transformation of substances, i.e. alchemy. The ascent, alone—the melting into light as an attempt to avoid going through the underworld—is not the way of tantra.

It is said that entering the path of tantra is more dangerous than taming and riding a tiger, and that one should never enter any kind of tantric work without a teacher. The implied reasons are that a teacher will observe your practice and recognize signs of maturity and signs of illusion, and act as a feedback mechanism. Also, the unspoken element is that a teacher is "divinely influential" in a student's life, when there is an honest, devotional relationship between the student and the teacher. Divine Influence is the necessary transformational mordant. Without that, you don't really transform anything. You just shift substances around. That is never spoken of because the impression might be left that one could simply rest on the teacher's influence, and really the path is too dangerous for that. One has got to keep one's eyes open and pay attention.

Any practice of higher esoteric techniques should only be utilized actively when the basic stuff is dealt with. If one's personality is predominantly negative, or depressive, or pessimistic, sexual tantra shouldn't be used. If one's relationships are always about protecting his territory, or about envy, fear and aggressiveness, then to even consider practicing sexual tantra is absurd, because what it will do is irritate whatever tendencies one has. It will magnify them a hundred times. But, likewise, if your relationships are full and celebratory, however; if a person celebrates God in the company of devotees, then they're ready to begin to study and investigate the practice of tantra. That too will be magnified. That too will be "irritated." Irritation can create a pearl in an oyster, or irritation can create destruction. It can be positive or negative. If you are full of God, the irritation created by sexual tantra will unleash energies and clarity and insights and revelation that won't get unleashed in other ways.

These tantric considerations might literally take years to become a consistent element in one's sexual practice. But wouldn't it be worth five or ten years of struggle and disappointment with conventional sex in order to have thirty years, or more, of sexual communion? If you want results—the transmutation of sexual energy from ordinary passion to a higher form of energy—you have to work. You have to give it discipline.

Monogamy is a recommended practice in this school because I believe that love breeds within a field of intimacy and union. Many teachers are inclined to split up relationships and discourage them from becoming permanent because they can tend to become obstructions to one's work—to overshadow one's relationship with the Divine. My approach, however, is just the opposite. I'm very much in support of long-term, lasting relationships and sometimes that creates difficulties because people have this "seven-year itch" or a "fourteen-year itch." Some men experience wanderlust from about age forty through about age sixty. They get very insecure.

People who live together in intimate circumstances for long periods of time, (and anything over seven years is getting to be a long period of time these days), will develop something with one another that they wouldn't develop under any other circumstances. You can't jump out of a long-term relationship into a new relationship that's hot and passionate and exciting, and hope to have what you had in the old relationship in less than seven years. It's impossible. (Of course your genitals wouldn't know that. But your genitals aren't who you are, thank God!) So, I'd fight pretty hard to keep a relationship alive that had developed something like that. Nothing is written in stone, however, so it may be that the relationship will end, but I also think we need to learn to make some sacrifices.

An Indian Sufi teacher, Bhai Sahib, once told his student, Irina Tweedie, that love needed to be built, and once built, the structure needed to be maintained and kept alive. Much of the work we do in our community, especially in the early years, is about building love—between mates and within families. Even with children you need to build love. It is not a given that just because you birthed a little being that looks and acts like you that you're going to necessarily love them. You need to build love and maintain it, and that's not easy. In fact this ability is unique in the universe. Yet it's worth whatever price you might have to pay for it—even if the price is physical health or peace of mind. It's that important.

It is also important to distinguish between false monogamy and true monogamy. In false monogamy you are limited to one person because you develop the kind of relationship that isolates the two of you against the world. So, for example, in that kind of relationship the guy comes home from work and Honey says, "Did you get the raise, babe?" And he says, "No, God damn it. They promoted somebody else over me." And Honey says, "What? What! They don't treat you right at that place. You ought to look for another job. Your boss doesn't appreciate you." They feed off one another and create this bubble to keep them apart from the world.

In true monogamy there is no urge on the part of either person to flirt or play seduction games or hunter games with other people. Partners in a true monogamous couple can still have intimate friendships with other men and women, and there is no obstacle to the primary relationship. That's the ideal scenario. The "love of the hunt" for the man is in his work, creativity, art, his passion for his wife and children. The woman nurtures her family, her man, home, environment, community, her art form. Then the whole world is actually one's oyster.

The Ongoing Saga of Relationship

Men and women in our times tend to have an interesting dynamic. When apart from one another, their sensitivity to the essential energy dynamic that exists between male and female is very acute. Separated, they can readily experience tremendous feelings of integrity, responsibility, and clarity towards each other. They can develop the clear intention of being together in a mood of service, compassion, generosity, and gentleness.

As long as they are not confronted by the superficial, five-sense stimuli, it is always much easier for them to "see" or instinctually sense the pure and perfect archetypal essentials of the other—male or female.

So, paradoxically, men and women intend to relate to one another based on the essential relationship of energy that each of them represent, but when they get together, ego tends to use the physical dynamic to create a circumstance that is completely selfish or self-centered, instead of relational.

Let me give you an example. They meet at the end of the day, full of intention towards elegance, sensitivity, and communion. The man walks in and, having a terrible and weird sense of humor, says to the woman who has been cooking an extraordinary meal for hours, "What stinks, honey?"

Then he looks at the roast in the oven and exclaims, "D-don't tell me that's the dog. My God, I was just getting to like that furry, little shit!"

Well, the woman is somewhat used to his sense of humor, so it is annoying, but she says, "Ha ha ha, isn't that funny. Just go get cleaned up and ready for dinner."

He says, "O.K." and doesn't think a thing about it, happily waltzing off to the bathroom, to wash his hands or more likely to admire himself in the mirror.

A few minutes later the man comes out and goes to sit down at the table. Now the woman says, "No, no, I want you to sit here," indicating a different chair from the one he is choosing.

He says, "Can't I sit here?"

She says "No, no, it's very important, you have to sit here."

Then he gives in, and sits down where the woman has directed him, but meanwhile he's getting a little bit annoyed too. "After all," he is thinking, "a man's home is supposed to be his castle, isn't it? And the king ought to be able to sit where the hell he wants, shouldn't he?"

At last she brings out the dinner and soon she too is waltzing, and maybe even singing around him, in the way happy and affectionate women do. She's taking care of him, mothering and doting. Well, there's nothing that makes a man angrier than when a woman trys to take care of him as if he were two years-old. So, as you can imagine, by the time dinner is over, both of them have got big agendas of issues. They are both annoyed, even though they're being polite to one another. But the tension is definitely building up.

While they were apart, they had the intention to be different in relationship to one another. Once together, the habitual and uninspected psychological trigger-mechanisms completely obscured the best of intentions.

A man may at times know what a woman wants, or how women want to be treated, or what the "Essential Woman" needs, and vice versa. Yet the dilemma is how to resolve the struggle between what we feel in sensitive and clear moments with the incredible power of ego to immediately blind us with its own devious intentions. (You shouldn't make any mistake about ego's intentions. Maybe "devious" is even too light a word. Ego's entire intention is to maintain its survival, and it will destroy anything that gets in its way! Anything—including the body itself! Many examples of suicide demonstrate this in psychologically predictable ways.)

Three things are particularly useful in working with this dichotomy, this dilemma: Understanding, Intention or Resolution, and the Discipline to pay the price. The first thing that we need to work on is a clear, precise understanding of the mechanics of habit — of how sex becomes not a pleasurable element of relationship, but a powerful tool for manipulation of self or others. This must include a recognition that change doesn't happen overnight, and that change and progress happen in the circumstances one is presently involved in, not somewhere else.

The second element of working with the dilemma of men and women has to do with cultivating the attitude that resolution will come through practice, experience, self-observation and the intention to be different. It does not come through some kind of extreme, "do-or-die," ascetic practice.

The third necessary element is the willingness to give attention and discipline—i.e., to make the resolution of this dilemma worth the price that needs to be paid. If every time you feel a bit lusty you "get laid," you will never deal with the issue of Right Relationship; you will never engage Real Masculinity and Real Femininity. You will never integrate the health and vitality of your own anima/animus. This kind of discipline and attention will only be worked out in a long-term, committed relationship.

When people bond with one another and reach a certain level of understanding with one another, it's like they're beautifully, exquisitely, romantically trapped together. The longer people live together in community, the longer you are together as a couple, the more bonded you become to one another, and the more it becomes a sobering consideration.

It's extremely sobering to wake up one morning with your mate sleeping beside you, to look at him or her, and genuinely realize the degree of bonding that exists between you, and the nature of it. It's also a realization that opens the heart. It is Real. It must be faced head on.

Our culture is full of role models of divorced people and single parents. What we lack are role models of dedicated, happy, alchemically-transformed couples, or other configurations. So, it often happens that people get into a relationship, saying they are "in love" and that the relationship is "forever" but psycholgically they think: "Well, if it doesn't work, what the hell."

If you understand and practice and become an apprentice within this body of knowledge, you will reach a point when you can't go back. You will never be able to go back to ordinary existence anymore. Many of you are tied to the Work in a way that is irrevocable. You can beat your head against the wall, desparately trying to find satisfaction in the old ways—in conventional sex, in T.V., or food, or any of the addictions and forms of self-indulgence. But you won't be able to. So why fight it? Don't be frustrated, then. Just surrender to it. There are greater joys in this Work than there are in stuffing yourself with food, or whatever.

A key word here is *apprenticeship*. If you read any literature about apprenticeship, or any of the magical literature about alchemy, you'll learn that no apprentice can ever go back. They never know that, however, until they've tried and failed. They don't realize it until it's too late. The results of this apprenticeship process are invaluable. If, at the end of a lifetime, you can say that you've drawn one real picture, written one real poem, genuinely nurtured one child, been a real friend or a real lover to one other person, it's worth anything. It's worth your looks, your money, your security, anything. Some of you know that and that's why you're here, and some of you aren't quite sure of that yet. But, that's what we're doing together in spiritual Work. We're in this to become human beings.

Natural Tantra = Organic Innocence

If you are going to practice tantra, it should be spontaneous, natural tantra; and if you love someone deeply enough, you will do tantra. If you are not selfish, if your own satisfaction doesn't come first, even if it's subconscious, you will discover tantra, naturally, in your relationships with your lover, and with your friends as well, since tantra practice is not limited to sex. It takes time. There are many ordinary hang-ups to get over, as you well know. But once you've gotten over those things, you'll discover tantra.

Our way as Bauls is not about developing the "observer" as they do in Tibetan tantra—i.e., training that aspect of mind to be absolutely objective, and completely detached. That's much too technical for us. It's too detached, too cool. Our way is about relaxing into Organic Innocence, not "technique-ing ourselves" into perfect control.

Many people begin to love someone and start to feel themselves losing control. They find themselves in a situation in which the other person is becoming their "master" in a certain sense, and that terrifies them. They see that the other is self-centered, and neurotic, as we all are, and they assume that he or she will abuse them, or will take them for granted. So they break off the relationship. They decide that it isn't worth it. I'm telling you, however, that no matter who the other person is, love transforms. If you are falling in love and you hold back because you are afraid it is bad for your spiritual Work, you may easily miss a very important consideration. My way is to suggest that you throw yourself into it. When you truly surrender in love there should be no fear of compromising your Work. Just surrender, and give it time too. Don't be in such a hurry—"Okay, I'll surrender, but...my partner had better change in two months or..." Remember what I've been saying about the need for long-term committment. Throw yourself into it and leave yourself in it, and you will transform yourself and that other person too.

When you are "sexing," just "sex." Don't be busy interpreting every sound, every movement that's going. Let your body do what it will. Don't interpret, fantasize, invalidate, criticize, condemn, be guilty, and all the other stuff that you typically do when you're sexing. You don't do that when you're seeing. When you're seeing, you're seeing. You aren't busy being guilty because you see. When you are just sexing you will find that you will transcend sex, literally.

Intercourse does not have to stop. You don't have to transcend intercourse, but you must transcend the usual, mechanical, habitual reasons for sex. Sex must become love, and then love must be transcended. What transcends love? God. Sex must turn into love, but to love you need the duality of lover and the beloved. And even that must be transcended. You must lose "the one who is loving." You must lose the one who is "in love." So, even sex that has been transformed into love, which is a beautiful thing, must also be transformed, because the lover must be lost. You who are the lover must lose yourself. <u>You must transcend love and become the very nature of creation itself</u>, which we call God. You must simply be what is unfolding as the Great Process of Divine Evolution. And if what is going on happens to be sexual intercourse, then that's what's going on. Simply be that. What must be transcended is not the form. What must be transcended is the search, i.e., the neurosis of genital absorption and exclusivity.

About Love—At Last

The word "love" is one that, generally, I can't ridicule enough. Yet it keeps coming up. I've tried often enough to replace it with sophisticated synonyms, but nothing exactly equals it to my satisfaction—not life, or reality, or truth, or suffering.

I resist, mightily, using the word "love," both because of psychological mechanisms associated with it, and due to the fact that it is so easily misunderstood. Just listen to how often "I love you" is said everywhere in the world, and ask yourself, "Is there honor in all of the relationships in which that word is used?" I don't mean only between lovers, but between parents and children also. How many parents casually say "I love you" to their children when there is no honor or respect there. You probably have known divorced people with children who left their children as soon as some good-looking member of the opposite sex came along. They justify it to themselves, well enough, "I'll make it up to the children later. I've got to leap upon this opportunity now." It seems to me that if the person you are dating is willing to let you do that, he or she isn't much of an opportunity! There must be honor for love to be present in relationships!

Admittedly, it takes a lot to be able to sacrifice in a circumstance of such magnitude. More than discipline, it takes integrity, honor. No amount of discipline replaces honor. And without honor, there is no love.

Another reason I resist that "L" word is that it's generally soaked with sentimentality—like how your heart melts, or your eyes become moist as you gaze at your mate or your child. Every single mood of what you call love is just crap as long as you are still separate from God.

You can't have love and be separate from God. "Well, I'm going to maintain my separation from God because, after all, I've got dreams and aspirations and things I have to do with my life. I need to be free and I need to be creative and I need to dance and sing and sew and make children and take care of my man, first. I'll have time for God when I've done all I need to do in my life. Then I'll be loving...."

No you won't. Maybe you'll be conventionally a little more moral and appropriate than most people, but love is something that cannot exist separate from God. As long as your "I" is functioning, as long as it's "you" who wants love, and "you" who is giving love, it's not love. It may be affection. It may be caring. It may be concern, consideration, understanding, sympathy, empathy—but love? No. Not Love. No matter how exalted you feel when your lover gives you a rose, it isn't love. It's exaltation, not love. Love cannot be present when you are separate from God.

It's very fashionable these days to approach love as if it were a commodity. We mistakenly think that ego is going to keep it's autonomy, and we're going to get love as the final gift for being "good." No way! You don't get love by being good. You get love by disappearing, by dissolving. As long as "you" exist, love won't. When "you" cease to exist, love will immediately exist. Just like that. "You" exist, no love...not even a little bit. You don't get a taste of love while you're alive, and then when you die and drop your body, finally get the whole meal because then you don't have to worry any more about desires and lust and greed. That's not the way it works.

It's a perfect equation, really. No self = love. Self = no love. There are no degrees. The first thing you have to do is to give up all your little i's because you aren't ever going to get to know who your "I" is as long as you've got a world war going on inside your psyche. First you have to bring all your little i's to a kind of center, so that your three centers (the intellect, the heart, and the moving center) are essentially sympathetic, and not functioning at cross-purposes. The recommended conditions of meditation, exercise, and study do that. Then, once you get that to feel like you are in a pretty high state most of the time, and you're detached, and you've got visions coming through, then you've got to give that up too. Finally, you've got to go through the world naked, free of an "I" that defends you, and protects you, and makes sure you're always right. As long as you attempt to dramatize and glorify your "I," you will never realize God. You will have no choice. Not a prayer! If you begin to be willing to give that up, the Work will proceed quickly. In fact, you'll fly through it. The crucifixion will be hard, but over soon.

Some of you have been hanging on the cross for years, and it's really your own fault. There is nothing to blame but your own perverse, stubborn refusal to surrender your "I." And it's just not true to say, "But I can't..." You can, but you're stubborn. Everybody is. So there you have it.

Life is so simple. Really there are only two things: the "I" and the transcendence of "I." Instead, we make this infinite range of intervening considerations, "What about life after death? When does the soul enter the body? Is abortion moral? What about men...women...relationships...life...death...sex...infinity? How long will 'General Hospital' be on T.V.? Why do the nurses on that show never grow old?"

Hey, maybe that's the answer to all of this. Maybe we all ought to enter the "T.V. world." We'd all be preserved just the way we are now and never grow old, and we'd have a nice life there.

Well, there you have it once again, hmmm?

Chapter Seven

✓

LONGING AND DEVOTION

I want to tell you the story of Rumi, who initiated the practice of the whirling dervishes. Rumi is well known also for writing volumes of poetry to God, addressed through his teacher, Shams-e Tabriz. It is said that he wrote over thirty-thousand verses, and the most striking feature of all his poetry is the communication of his longing for what he called "the Beloved."

Longing, practically speaking, is feeling the possibility of grasping what is impossible to grasp. Given who we are as human beings, as a race, the transformational process is like something that is "not supposed to happen." Yet the lives of many of the great mystics in all traditions is indicative that even though it's impossible, it has happened. There you have a valuable *koan*. Longing for the impossible as a possibility, not as a reality, is where a lot of the mystical poetry of all ages comes from—in the Sufi literature, the Hindu, the Christian mystical poetry of St. John of the Cross, and others.

Rumi was a very well known theologian. He was a great scholar and had a big following. In fact, he was recognized as one of the greatest Islamic thinkers of the age. But, despite his great success, a growing dissatisfaction was starting to work in his life. He'd read all the mystical poetry and had an intellectual appreciation of it. Like many people, he knew what it meant in a technical sense, but he questioned deeply about whether all his confidence was just a mask, and that he might really be missing the heart of it. As this dissatisfaction grew he became increasingly more irritated and tense in his life. He was "primed"—as they say in the business.

Just at that time a wandering dervish came into town, a man named Shams-e Tabriz, which means friend of God. He was wearing rags and was dirty and disheveled when Rumi and his group of students first laid eyes on him as they walked through the streets discussing some scholarly subject. "Just another dirty beggar...," Rumi assumed. As a sign of offering from his great benediction, Rumi reached into his pocket, took out a coin, and threw it on the street for Shams to pick up. Then he told the beggar to step aside so that he could move on. Shams laughed, but did as commanded, and Rumi and his students walked away.

It was only a momentary encounter, but something had been touched in Rumi. Despite all his sophistication the scholar was haunted by the memory of the eyes of this dirty beggar. He just couldn't get this man out of his mind, and became more and more annoyed because the image started to interfere with his lucidity of thought, his ability to be just who he'd been all his life. It got so bad that Rumi found it difficult to sleep, and wanted to run out into the streets and see this man again. He didn't even know the beggar's name, and since the town was always filled with such wanderers, Rumi convinced himself that to go out searching was a stupid thing to do and would probably make him look like an ass. Instead, he stayed at his work and became more and more anxious and short-tempered with his students. When, on the next day, the vision of Shams was even stronger, Rumi could not stand it any longer, and went out walking the streets.

Rumi became afraid. He feared he was going mad. Never before had he had such a problem with his mind, and yet never before had he felt so ecstatic, like at any moment he might discover the greatest secret, the greatest treasure.

From out of nowhere, Shams walked in front of him, and looked Rumi straight in the eye. Immediately Rumi fell to the ground, weeping, and lost in a state of ecstasy. Finally it dawned on him that this is what he'd been reading about in all the mystical literature. This is what he'd been waiting for all his life, but had never really known before.

Realizing the chance of a lifetime, Rumi left everything and went to be with Shams. He told his students that he was taking a sabbatical and began to ignore his formal responsibilities and habitual work, and this made his students very angry.

"I've been your teacher for years," Rumi said to them, "but I never knew what I was teaching you. I had only book learning. But now my teacher has come, so. . .bug off suckers!"

Rumi had fallen so in love with this wandering dervish that everything in his life started to fall away, except for the poetry he began to write for Shams.

As you can imagine, Rumi's students didn't like this situation at all. They thought that Shams had hypnotized their teacher; that Shams was a magician, or a devil who must be destroyed. They began to create a plan to do just that. They threatened him with violence. They offered him money to leave, but Shams simply laughed in their faces.

One night, as one story goes, Rumi's students invited Shams to come to the roof of one of their dwellings, on the pretense of needing to discuss a problem with him. When Shams arrived, they stabbed him to death. Rumi learned what had happened and, faced with the prospect of living without his beloved teacher for the rest of his life, he went mad. The cost of his longing was the disintegration of all illusions. This madness turned into a life of devotion, one of the expressions of which was the whirling dance.

The intensity of longing that was the result of Rumi's relationship to Shams is often used to describe the most optimal relationship to God that one can have.

+ + +

When Rumi was ready, Shams showed up. When a student has longing, nothing, no matter what it is, can stand in the way of the teacher's feeding that longing, since genuine longing creates a reciprocal feeding process. That is, the student's longing becomes a very refined and necessary food for the teacher.

Of course, the bastardized forms of longing that we have tended to assume, like false holiness and idol worship, must be eliminated before the real longing can provide its essential quality. It is very easy to give desires a high definition, and thereby confuse these with genuine longing. If your longing is for a car, or an apartment you can't have, it's fairly obvious that this type of longing is not the real thing. If you say that you're longing for God, however, it's easy to fool yourself. People can create all sorts of fantasies around that. They can easily use it to avoid facing the hard-core facts of reality. But, with real longing you don't avoid life. Some of the greatest Sufis who have written about this notion of longing were the most practical people. They had families, they had jobs, they were responsible. They took care of things, were charitable, gentle, and honest. On the other hand, the Sufis also talk about a place called the Tavern of Ruin. This is a place for people whose taste of longing has begun to "ruin" them, completely, the way Rumi was ruined by his longing for Shams.

Ordinarily, we practice, we mature, we become more grounded in our experiences, we have less confusion…and all of that works in a progressive way. But, then there's a kind of "point of no return" in which one falls into the heart of God in a way that involves a complete severing of any distraction or fantasy that one has about life, reality, the illusion of things. It is a kind of permanent severing of ego. From this point on it is not possible for ego to be autonomous or independent again. At that level, everything is irrelevant except the Divine, completely. The Work itself cuts you loose, at that point. It no longer demands of you the same responsibilities. You just get a different job.

There's a story in the New Testament about Jesus that can illustrate what I'm saying here. Jesus came to Bethany to visit the home of his friends Lazarus, Martha and Mary. Lazarus greeted him and brought him into the house. When Jesus sat down, Mary seated herself at his feet and began to weep. Her tears were so plentiful that she washed Jesus' feet with them. In the meantime, sister Martha was running around baking bread and getting dishes ready. She was in a flurry of activity to attend to all the things that needed to be done for this important occasion, and she soon started to get annoyed because Mary wasn't helping. So, Martha barked at her, or at Jesus, saying, "Come on. Get your ass off the pillow and get up here and help me get things ready."

But, Jesus rebuked Martha for this. He said, "You have one job and she has another and she really loves me. You have the right form, but she really has the heart of devotion." (I'm paraphrasing here.)

Devotion to the teacher *is* devotion to God. Often people will say they are devoted to God and deny any form of personal devotion to a teacher. They claim that it is really a distraction.

It takes a tremendous vulnerability to be in a devotional relationship to the Divine. It is extremely uncomfortable, unless one happens to be born disposed to this sort of thing. I certainly wasn't. My own tendency had always been towards the extreme side of coolness. When I was young my aunts and uncles and cousins would all come to visit, and they always wanted to kiss me and hug me. I would shy away from them. Everyone thought I had the coldest heart of any child in the family. If I hadn't come to this work, I probably would have lived my whole life with an entire dimension of my being—the heart—unexpressed and unripened.

As the organism matures, there is a pull to an objective form of devotion. However, most people *feel* that movement and simply express it by becoming disgustingly sentimental and emptily romantic. They get misty-eyed and start sighing at the sight of lovers walking down the street hand in hand—"Ah, isn't that beautiful"! But, that is not a response of true devotion. The nature of the heart is not just to feel emotion, but to respond to the qualities of adoration, majesty, glory, beauty, faithfulness.

Gurdjieff (a great Russian mystic with a very large following, particularly in Europe and America), was very specific about the fact that if, at his funeral, anyone was expressing a particular form of outward emotion, they could not possibly have gotten what it was that he was teaching. In fact, Gurdjieff's students only once reported seeing him express outward emotion. That story is a remarkable one.

Certain students were designated by Gurdjieff to go out and teach and represent the Work. Since none of these students was complete in his or her own work, they were sent out with the understanding that when they needed more input, or more help, they would return. Sometimes Gurdjieff would go out to them himself, but either way it was clear that their relationship to Gurdjieff was that of student to teacher, and that this would continue to progress and deepen.

One of these students, a man named Orage, was sent to America where he developed a very large following. He was quite charismatic and personally powerful. The problem was that Orage's students were extremely enthusiastic about him, yet most of them had no idea who Gurdjieff was. So, Orage raised money and arranged for Gurdjieff to visit him and to work with the students he had collected, and the Master agreed.

When Gurdjieff arrived he was taken to a meeting of Orage's students. Taking one look around the room, Gurdjieff began to speak, saying that it was obvious to him that Orage had been teaching them completely wrong. He said he could feel that none of them knew what they were doing, and that all the work they had done had been worthless.

Gurdjieff's teaching method was very harsh. He was extremely strong with his own students and often thrust them into situations that were not only shocking, but exceptionally strenuous on their bodies and emotions. He was a hard, hard taskmaster. In this instance he called Orage a false master, telling the new students that they had a charlatan for a teacher, and that Orage had abused the responsibility he had been given.

Then, Gurdjieff told the group that he himself was the teacher—Orage's teacher—and that he knew the Work, while Orage didn't. Anyone who really wanted to do the Work, Gurdjieff said, had to become his student directly, and in fact had to sign a statement swearing that they would completely sever all relationships with Orage—not see him, not speak to him, not read anything he had written. Nothing. Gurdjieff arranged that people should bring their signed statements to him at his apartment on the following afternoon. Anyone who didn't, he said, was finished as far as the Work was concerned.

Well, as you can probably imagine, the group was thrown into absolute turmoil. A few of the people who recognized Gurdjieff's seniority immediately decided that they would sign. Others ran to Orage asking, "What should we do? You are the teacher, tell us whether to sign or not." Some asked him, "What does this mean? What are you going to do now? Will you still teach?" But, true to Orage's seniority in the Work, he refused to give advice to anyone. He simply told them, "Do what you have to do."

The following day, in the middle of the afternoon, Orage walked into Gurdjieff's apartment. He moved towards the Master, stood directly in front of him and gave Gurdjieff the signed statement swearing to have nothing whatsoever to do with Orage, or with anyone who had anything to do with Orage from then on, and acknowledging that Gurdjieff was his exclusive teacher. Gurdjieff took the paper, and without any change of expression walked toward the kitchen, and, once in there, wept. This was the only time that any of his students ever saw an expressive display of emotion by him. Yet, I don't think it can be said that Gurdjieff was a man who was not full of devotion and feeling.

Genuine devotion, devotion to truth, is full of passion and intensity, full of life and juice and energy. Many Zen masters are good examples of this. The first time that poet Gary Snyder met D.T.

Suzuki, Snyder was very young and enamored with the Zen literature and the Buddhist teachings. Given his age and his highly refined and sensitive intelligence but simple lack of experience, he was quite impulsive. He saved his money with one goal in mind—to travel to Japan and visit Suzuki at the temple in which he was residing. When he finally got there, of course he was very excited. Suzuki greeted Snyder and his friend, and very graciously invited them to join him in the temple for his practice. They were thrilled. Imagine, seeing this great man at his practice—this man who embodied for them the goal of realization.

Suzuki walked into the temple, and the men followed. He proceeded to light candles and incense, and to worship the Buddha shrine. Now, Snyder and his friend were shocked by what they saw. "What is this?" they asked the great master. "What is this worship of idols? You're supposed to burn the Buddha, kill the Buddha...." (Being such enthusiastic students they had read all the great Zen stories.)

Suzuki turned, and very sweetly and gently smiled at them. "You burn the Buddha," he said. "I'll worship the Buddha."

Of course, what wasn't said was that Suzuki had "killed" the Buddha years ago. He had already realized nonduality. Because of that he was truly available to worship, to express real devotion. To "kill the Buddha" is only the first step. Life doesn't go on by living on the first step, however. One needs to move ahead—always—or one dies.

Literally, it is true that there is no separation between us and God—that there is only God. God is not some "thing" or some "one" outside of ourselves that needs to be looked for, prayed to, etc. It is also true that human beings have organic dispositions towards a variety of expressions of thought, feeling and physical activity, and that there is a quality of the human being that cannot be satisfied outside of a certain mood of devotion or adoration.

But, then the question arises: Devotion to who? Adoration to what? We will need to build up to the answer to that question.

The first point is this: It is impossible to know or experience real devotion unless you are already consumed by the realization of nonduality—the realization of enlightenment. Any devotion felt or expressed outside of a tacit presumption that the Divine is all there is. . .may be completely sincere, and pure in its motivation; it may be positive and free of violence and negativity; and yet, it is not true devotion—no matter what it looks like, no matter how it feels.

One can feel true devotion for a moment when one experiences union with that which is "All." But, the minute the experience of nonduality leaves and one is back again in his typically neurotic state, whatever is then expressed is just desperate or frustrated mimicry of real devotion.

The second point about devotion has to do with the profound consideration of the personal Beloved. The Sufis define this as an external, ultimate, and personalized form of God. They give the Beloved the perfect human qualities and express their relationship to that in poetry. Usually the poetry will describe the unimaginable beauty of the Beloved's skin, the hair, the ringlets of the hair, the Beloved's eyes and lips. . .every quality of the face is given the most exceptional and majestic capacity to elevate the viewer into ecstasy.

In Hindu poetry, when they speak about the Beloved, Krishna, most of it is very erotic. Many poems will refer to Krishna's bare chest, and how his skin feels when pressed against the breasts of the Gopis, and the sweat of the engagement of their meetings. But, in the Sufi poetry, just the face and perhaps the neck is described, as if anything more than that would be just too much to bear sensually.

The heat or mood of this Sufi poetry is not that of *having* the Beloved, or being *united* with the Beloved, but rather of the sweetness of *longing* for that which you know and feel to be perfect, and yet can never attain.

A man once told me an unbelievable story which relates to this. "I looked for a long time," the man related, "and finally I found the woman of my dreams. She was perfect. The minute we met both of us knew that this was it. It! We sat together and talked for hours, even though nothing needed to be said between us. Then she invited me up to her apartment and on the way she told me that she was really unattached to many things, but the thing she most loved in her life was her dog.

"Well, when we got to her place I met her big, black dog, and he was very friendly. So while this woman of my dreams was in the bathroom I started playing with the dog. I found a ball and began throwing it, and each time I did, the dog would run and get the ball and bring it back to me. Great fun. I liked the dog, and we hit it off right away, with no problems.

As we played the dog got more excited, and I got more excited. I bounced the ball hard and it went right out the window, and right out after it went the dog. This woman's apartment was on the fifth floor.

"It took a few moments for me to comprehend what had happened. Then, all of a sudden the reality struck me. I got up. I left her apartment while she was still in the bathroom, and I never saw her again. But I have always longed for her, feeling acutely the loss of the only ideal relationship I ever glimpsed."

It's a funny story, but a very powerful one. Can you get it? At the time this man was about twenty-five years-old. He had finally met the woman of his dreams. Now, for the rest of his life, everything he will see or do will be touched by his memory of that moment, by the memory of the last time he saw this woman's face.

The Sufi poetry is not about seeing the Beloved again and again, or getting to know the Beloved more each time. It's about the one real glimpse, and the knowing that follows on that. That's it! Beauty so unearthly, so perfect, so unattainable, that you just know the instant you get that glimpse that this is all you've ever hungered for. Then, it is gone forever.

In the Baul tradition of Bengal, in India, they speak about the Beloved as being "the man of the heart." *Maner manush* is the

Bengali term for it. They relate to the Beloved not as one to be found outside, but as one who stands in the human heart waiting to release the heart to ecstasy. This is the tradition to which I most closely associate. It is relatively contemporary, meaning that it's merely several hundred years old. In India, the only people who accept the Bauls as being anything other than just thieves and liars and beggars are the Indian Sufis.

It is longing for the Beloved that will transform the devotee, not having the Beloved. It is very important to understand this in principle. There is no such thing as perfection. Yet, the human being in his or her ultimate expression cannot be ultimately satisfied or full without realizing perfection in some form. All art is an attempt to actually manifest or produce perfection, but, a work of art is shit. Every work of art is. In the moment of the artist's glimpse of the Beloved, perfection is brought down into the human realm. The work of art that attempts to embody that vision in form is just what is left over after the vision. The *Pieta* as a work of art, or Bach's Masses may inspire ecstasy in someone who is listening to the work or viewing the statue, but if one really gets the essence of the artist in that work one will be given an insatiable hunger, not satisfaction. In the moment of ecstasy there is satisfaction, but then all things pass, including ecstasy. True ecstasy always leaves something in its wake which is not simply egotistical hunger, something which is more than the desire to be outside of suffering. In the moment of true ecstasy, ego forgets.

Being desires ecstasy because after ecstasy one remembers. The ecstasy itself is just an experience like any other experience, but it is a doorway. It's value lies in where it is a doorway to, and not in the intensity of the feelings of pleasure that it is.

There is no such thing as perfection, and yet there *is* such a thing as true devotion—the desire to worship perfection in the personal form. It is a paradox. There is no such thing as perfection, and yet all is perfect. That's what the realization of nonduality is—that all of life, all of this that you see around you right now, is perfect. But, this must be *realized*, not just held or used as a concept. To realize that all is perfect is different from *trying* to relate to life as if it is all perfect. That would be maddening—"You mean that bastard who cut me off on the highway is perfect? No way!"

The Beloved is exclusively human. The Baul idea of the "man in the heart" is literal imagery related to human perfection. So, the question arises, is one's devotion directed to a literal "thing" or "object?" The answer to that is "No." Absolutely not. Is the devotion then directed toward an empty ideal, a kind of archetypal symbol? Here again the answer is "No." How can this be?

The Buddhists have an aspect of *dharma* that is contained in the statement: "Emptiness is form, form is emptiness." So, to the question: "Is there a literal Beloved somewhere? Does the Beloved (the ideal of perfection that is impossible), have a form?" No, it doesn't. It is emptiness. But then, emptiness is form. "This body that I inhabit, that you inhabit, is this empty?" We certainly don't feel that it is. This is clearly form. It feels, it thinks, it emotes, it can be defined and distinguished over and against other forms. It is clearly in relationship in a temporal, spatial way. Yet to realize one's enlightenment is to realize that this—this body of yours—is absolute emptiness too.

Form is emptiness, emptiness is form. Whether the Beloved is the "Friend" of the Sufis, the Ultimate companion…or whether the Beloved is the "Man of the Heart" of the Bauls…or whether the Beloved is Krishna, or Jesus for the contemplative Christian whose form of practice is to take Jesus as spouse or mate and worship in that form—it is all the same. What we are devoted to… what we worship or adore is the experience of union with all that is. We are in worship to nonduality. Such worship literally "kills" the Buddha, and destroys the notion or the image of God as Savior, or "other."

For the first several hundred years after Buddha's death it was prohibited to make images of him. The earliest images were not of the Buddha's face, but rather of his footprints—footprints full of symbols that implied all that Buddha represented. A similar thing occurred in Christianity. The predominant Christian practice in the first few centuries after Christ was the "Prayer of the Heart" or the "Jesus prayer." Its expression in the human body, however, was not to Jesus the Nazarene but rather to the Christ of Being. When one realizes the practice of the heart, one's devotion to Jesus becomes absolute. Devotion to Jesus is not defined by superficial notions of Jesus as the son of God, or Jesus the miracle worker or healer, but to Jesus as the paradoxical Christ. There is no rational Christ. That a human being could also be a Christ, or a Buddha, is totally inexplicable. That resolution can only be made outside of the domain of time and space, outside of the domain of duality. Within duality it is literally impossible.

Once one stands upon the foundation of realizing one's already present enlightenment (since there is never really any separation from God, there is never unenlightenment either), only then is one available to the possibility of devotion. If one is responsible with integrity for what the realization of enlightenment means, the body will grow spontaneously and naturally into a space in which devotion will arise all by itself—uncalled for and usually quite unexpected.

To realize one's enlightenment is to have and become what I call "Draw-no-conclusions-mind." When that happens there is no longer any question or problem about to what or to whom one is devoted. One simply feels devotion and knows, and follows instinct. At the same time one recognizes that one has returned to duality, yet still within the context of nonduality—as contrasted with seeking nonduality from inside the context of duality. Then there is not only the *realization* of truth, but the practical expression of truth in the world.

And that's all for now.

Chapter Eight

ABOUT COMMUNITY

It is my definitive intention to create community and a specific culture, not to collect individual students. By culture I mean something that encompasses a complete education—about childbearing, about conception, pregnancy, birth, ongoing education, death, everything. A culture sets the whole context for how one lives one's life—especially one's relationship to art and the creation of art. It is important to realize that one's own body is an art form and that art is expressed in dress, in cleanliness, in the diet and food, in one's bodily movement.

The culture of an effective community should include the handicapped, the non-handicapped, the emotionally disturbed, the non-emotionally disturbed (if there is such a thing), infants, children, adults, the elderly. A community includes all those, not just the young, healthy people who can run.

I see the formation of tribal community as the most powerful cultural manifestation for resisting the dehumanizing elements of the world culture-at-large. Yet, I know that it is extraordinarily difficult to expect people from a variety of backgrounds and personal preferences to come together and build tribal community. But that's the ideal. That is the goal that my personal Work is designed to effect.

Typically, in Western society, the great fear that people have about community is that they will lose their individuality. And that's a valid fear. In this big mass of undulating humanity, in general, and in many religious communities, and certainly in most political communities, in particular, that is exactly what happens. Political community effectively requires that people lose their individuality or else there is no community. In a real tribal community, however, the primacy of the community is tacitly recognized by all the individuals within it. Yet, this recognition is not to the exclusion of the individuality of the members. In such cultures, highly defined and strong individuality exists exactly coincident with community, and there is no conflict.

We can't imagine such a situation. In the West we don't have any direct experience with real community. We may have read about tribal cultures, or perhaps even travelled among them, but for the most part we don't have adequate examples. All we know is the nuclear family as community—Mom, Dad, and the two-and-a-half kids or so—and there couldn't be a more political community than that! Or we may view the "corporate family" as community. But, that too is a very bad example of community. It is no wonder then that we can't imagine how one could be in community and still maintain some individuality.

If our interest is in spiritual community we may say to ourselves, "Well, this school has many recommendations—meditating daily, studying daily, exercising daily, and lots of other minor things. But if I'm going to be an individual and I don't feel like meditating, how am I going to maintain my own independence?"

Look—to maintain your individuality doesn't mean that you never do a job that you'd rather not do, especially if you need the money to live. Right? It's simply a matter of priorities. It's the same thing in a spiritual community. You meditate everyday, you study everyday, you exercise everyday, *and* you maintain the same rasty, nasty attitude you always have. No problem! (Except maybe to the other people you live with. But really, no problem!) The idea of individuality, the pursuance of one's art, pursuance of the things that one enjoys, and so on, like all things in life, sometimes needs to be compromised for higher necessities.

I've sacrificed certain joys in my life just because other things were more necessary. I've had to utilize my time in other ways—ways that were simply more important than the things I used to do...things I loved, enjoyed and appreciated. So, if the ideal of community, and the communion that is the result of that, is important enough, you'll just give up eating meat, and drinking coffee and beer as often as you like. That's all. That's not submerging your individuality in some great community soup. It's simply making a sensible choice. The only way you can make truly sensible choices is out of true individuality.

In our community in Arizona there are currently about thirty adults living on the Ashram, and probably half of them participate in the recommended practice, regularly. As I see it, the point is to practice out of your individuality because you've made the choice to practice, not to submit yourself with constant resistance to some higher authority. I could make a rule that says, "Anybody who doesn't meditate everyday can't live on the Ashram." But I haven't. Yet. So the fear that one will lose one's individuality is first of all unfounded, and secondly, *where that fear comes from* is one of the things that this Work will help clarify for you. (Excuse my insolence, but some of you would do well to surrender what you call your individuality. Believe me, you'd be a lot healthier for it.) Some people hang on to such twisted, unhappy, personality structures as some kind of a sign of their individuality. How bizarre!

I find structure to be very valuable, as long as we use the structure intelligently and not allow it to become our new parent. On my own I've tried to learn to practice martial arts, and I found that in a highly structured class I could learn ten times what I could learn if I were only practicing on my own. Alone I couldn't make my own friction. In class, however, I had the black belt instructor on my back, making me work. (Literally, he had me lying on my back, and in that position moving up and down the mat.) I definitely wouldn't do that to myself.

A spiritual school serves in much the same way. There are "tortures," sure, but it's good! Basically, the point of having a group is not that everybody has to do everything exactly the same, and if they don't they get their hands slapped. The group is a structure in which the Divine Influence can be made available. We as individuals need to recognize its value and maintain relationship with the Influence. We don't have to agree with all the stuff that goes on in the group…all the stuff that other people exhibit. And there will be a lot of *stuff*. There's no question about it!

Any structure has it's problems; it's just built into the dynamic. But, "no-structure" has more problems. Even Krishnamurti had grade schools and high schools based (i.e. "structured") on his definition of no-structure. To be able to move through life without structure, one first *needs structure* to effect that movement. People hear that principle and they say, "Okay, that sounds good. If I become your student when will I get it so that I can go out with no structure?"

My response to that is, "I don't know."

You have to try it out for yourself. Most of my students have been students for a long time, since there is not a lot of turnover in this school. Yet, if you observe these long-time students I don't think you will find that they wear this association as a burden or a handicap. A structure is able to effectively gather resources together, in a spiritual way, not just by some superficial networking. Structure is able to magnify energy. For example, take several disconnected people—they will have a certain power. If you connect all those people, let's say three people, the power will not be three times as great, rather it will be closer to thirty times as great.

The community is like a body, and the Influence is like the circulation, the blood-flow, in the body. And that is both wonderful, and not so wonderful. In one sense, any benefit to one cell in the body benefits the whole body. Disease, on the other hand, can also influence the whole body. In a healthy body, when infection begins, right away healing elements are sent to the source of the infection to contain it so that it doesn't infect the whole. The community is like that. This body is not free from illness, but the benefit of being a part of the body is that all the resources of the whole are available to fight one's illness. It is important to remember, however, that the body is just the body. It's not the Spirit. It serves a purpose for a certain number of years, and then when it ceases to serve it's purpose, it goes away.

One leaves the structure when the structure has become useless. . .when one doesn't need the structure anymore. One can also leave because the body has rejected it. (When a corporation doesn't need something it tries to put it into the archives forever. It gives you a gold watch.) When the body no longer needs something, like hair or teeth, it just loses them. The teeth don't say, the way some people are known to do, "Well, I've got the teaching now, I think I'll go start another body." When a lizard loses its tail to a bird, the tail doesn't become another lizard. The lizard grows another tail. This is useful to recognize.

My goal for this community is that it be an organic structure, completely—one which has its own knowledge, and functions on its own innate intelligence, meaning the intelligence of the Influence. An organic structure knows exactly what is so, and what it needs to do. The body knows when to breathe, for instance, or when the heart should beat. A church, on the other hand, is what you get when you take an organic structure and start putting on it the things that you think will make it "better." For example, we have a very distorted view of progress. In the U.S., "progress" means taking a woman in labor for childbirth, putting her on a table, putting her feet up in stirrups, giving her a shot in the back so she doesn't feel anything, and then somehow pulling the child out. That's supposed to be progress…as if women didn't know how to have babies before we had hospitals, and shots and X-rays, and all this other stuff.

Another example: In India, they don't have Western toilets. They just have holes in the ground and you have to squat or stand, but that's the way you go to the bathroom. The first time I tried it I just couldn't believe how natural it was. My whole body changed in its eliminations. I was amazed. Progress in India may be to set aside one place where everyone can squat rather than having people squat all over the jungle. But, for the Western mind, progress is to put up this structure—the toilet—and then to retrain the body to use it properly. That's assuredly a sign that we think we've got more intelligence than the body does innately.

Certainly, however, despite my aim for a thoroughly organic structure, the community is not that entirely. People still get into positions of power and then abuse that power in little ways. There are elements of the structure that are not mature yet. That's what we all work for. But, then again, just what is perfect? We all work towards perfection. We can't expect to walk into a community and simply find perfection, or threaten to walk out if it isn't perfect. We need to give it our juice. We need to give it our vision!

In an organic structure one never needs to decide on timing. The structure itself takes care of it. You have a flower, for instance, one full of seeds. The seeds don't need to say to the flower, "Okay, we're ready. Throw us to the air. Now…Come on"! That all just happens, very spontaneously and very naturally. That's the ideal structure. But, because the mind is something that is added to a basic organic structure, it's difficult for human beings to create a structure that is organic. Actually, that is every human being's destiny—to work towards the creation and to be a part of an organic structure. And I repeat, this in no way suppresses the individual's desire to be an individual.

An organic structure, in human terms, will not define, or eliminate, individual differences in taste, in preference, in artistic temperament, in emotional disposition. A real organic structure will not make everything the same—smooth and nice. It can't. But a mind-structure will. A mind-structure will make a corporation in which everybody wears the same clothes, uses the same language, watches the same movies. A mind-structure will legislate that everybody has sex once a week at 7 P.M. on Thursday night, and if you miss it, too bad, you'll have to wait until next week!

Working with structures that are made up of human beings one always gets to confront the weaknesses in the structure—the tendencies of human beings in positions of authority to abuse their power, and all kinds of other things. Nevertheless, we need to be a bit stubborn, and have some discipline, and just keep trying. Keep trying to bring a real, organic intelligence to the structure instead of just mental intelligence.

I think there are communities that have actually achieved organic intelligence, but sometimes it has been based on the teacher's power. Then, when the teacher dies, the power goes. Sometimes the teacher carries that for the community, and for me that's not good enough. I do carry a lot for the community, but my aim, my vision for the community, is that it become an organic structure without me having to carry it. This is very rare in human history. Not a rare vision—just a rare actuality.

Real Community—A Culture of Holiness

If the foundation upon which one attempts to build a sacred life is rotten, sooner or later the sacred life will get so heavy it will just collapse the foundation and everything will go with it. My use of the language may give you the impression that holiness is the last thinks on my mind. Quite the contrary. For me, a life that is not a life of holiness is not a life. The idea of living the rest of my life in a culture free of holiness is so disgusting as to be absolutely unacceptable.

In the first couple of years of my work I attempted to create a structure of holiness. In my naiveté I didn't realize the relationship between the foundation and the structure. I found that we created a lot of laughter, a lot of aggressive activity, and a lot of proselytizing. But, as time went on, it became clear that there was no transformation going on. False holiness can be kind of fun, if you've never seen it before. But, it gets very tiring, very fast. My attempt now is to create a culture of true holiness, and the students who study with me cleave to the same ideal. Some recognize the difficulty of it, and are genuinely willing to work until that's what we get. For them, as for me, there is no other acceptable option.

In a process of spiritual transformation there's a tremendous amount of stress and friction which somehow needs to be resolved. It doesn't necessarily need an outlet, but something needs to be done with it.

Often the friction shows up as tense emotions and strong moods, and so on. If you look at most spiritual communities, their environments are exactly like the environments that create psychosomatic illnesses. One of the more subtle distinctions, however, is that while stress ordinarily produces illness, if used properly it will produce something else. In isometric exercises, for instance, it is actually the resistance and tension that builds the muscles.

It is not that people doing intense spiritual work never get sick. They do. Sometimes we just miss a certain connection, or take too much in. If the circumstances of spiritual Work were not designed to produce transformation, they'd produce almost constant illness. One of the reasons that most schools have intentional practices like meditation and exercise and diet is because the practices act as absorptive sources for the effects of the stress. The friction of spiritual Work can actually build transformation as an alternative to expressing itself in sickness.

In my own work I am quite capable of being alone and enjoying my own company, isolated from community. At the same time, my spiritual work has always been in a group, with a school, with a teacher. In community there is an already established structure of people working at all different levels. Within that there is a shared experiential realization of the frustrations of knowing something and yet not being able to live what you know all the time—this issue of instant enlightenment versus gradual enlightenment. Instant enlightenment is like when somebody first hears the truth and immediately knows that it is true. All the rest of their spiritual work then, which could take a lifetime, is about being able to live that with consistency. You work hard, and you practice and then you walk home and there's this man or woman there, and in that moment it can easily happen that your practice goes right out the window. But, over time, if you maintain your intention and you have support and help, and if you're reminded enough, you grow into genuine relationship. I don't think there is any substitute for the company and expertise of other people who have had these same experiences and moved a little beyond them.

In *Aikido, Judo,* and some other forms of martial arts, there is a principle that's stated as, "Give in so as to conquer." What that may mean in community is that you allow other people their ego games as a way of drawing them out. Then, when their trust and vulnerability are called forth it can then be turned back on the ego games. That can be a very valuable learning.

We have to be patient and keep working hard. Over time we approach the ideal. I think a school, a community, is even more important than a teacher in one sense. We're all already enlightened, so to recognize enlightenment is really quite simple. But, to express that enlightenment every day in ordinary activity—that's the real Work, and that is what community is for.

Chapter Nine

ON SURRENDER AND THE
LAW OF SACRIFICE

Typically, when people get involved in spiritual work they become interested in the concepts of enlightenment, or liberation, or freedom. They feel the First Law of the Buddha—that all life is suffering—and they seek this work to be free of that suffering. For them, freedom means no restrictions, no bounds, an infinite number of choices. They want not just the world, but the whole universe, as their playground.

My experience is that in real freedom there are no choices. . .that real freedom is only present when there is "no one" to make choices. My first book is called *Spiritual Slavery*. [Editor's note: *Spiritual Slavery* is no longer in print.] In that book I expressed the essence, or underlying principle, of all the work that I do, i.e., when one surrenders to God one is moved by other than one's own personal attractions and conscious perceptions of who one is. Rather, in every instance one is moved by the Will of God. Within that, in every instant, and under every circumstance, there is only one optimal expression for each cell of creation. Anything less than that is simply the expression of ego.

Ego thinks that if it got enlightened then it could do anything it wanted in any moment and it would not have to function in a lawful way. But, that is not the case. The more submitted to the Will of God one is, the less laws there are, but the more absolute the laws become. In the world of normal activity, for instance, there are laws about speed limits, and laws about embezzlement, and laws about misrepresentation, and so on. But, to the laws of nature, these laws of man are totally irrelevant. Storms and earthquakes, lightning and volcanoes—what do they care for private property, to the injunction to "Keep Off The Grass?"

There is a hierarchy of laws, but the highest law, the law of God, is a law of Sacrifice. No other laws can stand in the face of that one. There are no options to it. Let me explain this as simply as I can. The nature of an ecological system is that everything in the system is fed on by something in the system, and in turn, feeds on something in the system. And human beings are no exceptions. The Law of Sacrifice means that we are all "food" for something higher.

When you begin to function in relationship to that Law, it doesn't matter whether or not you refuse to "be food" (to be consumed in the service of a higher process), you're going to be "eaten" anyway. The important thing to know is that you can either "go" graciously, making yourself the most elegant meal for that which eats you, or you can go kicking and screaming and complaining and protesting all the way.

Werner Erhard, the founder of est, and the Forum, often used the statement: "The chalk has already hit the floor." What he meant was this. If you have a piece of chalk and you drop it, even though there is a gap in time, the chalk has already hit the floor the minute you've released it. The implications are that the law of gravity is an absolute law within this plane of time and space. Once the chalk leaves your fingers, assuming there is a clear channel, i.e. no obstacles in the way and no extra-dimensional interception, the chalk has become the property of the law of gravity. Whereas before that, the chalk was the property of the law of whatever you wanted to do with it muscularly. So too, within our relationship to the Divine, there are laws. If we are able to release ourselves to those laws, they will work without obstruction, and the end result will be already assured from the moment that our release takes place. It is very important, therefore, to know what the laws are and how to release oneself to them.

The mind will be a spectacular excuse-maker. It is extremely sophisticated. The most antagonistic prospect the mind can face is not to function under its own power, but instead to be at the effect of another law. Even if functioning under its own power is in complete opposition to the Divine, the mind doesn't care as long as it is operating under its own power. That's the way the ego views things. Therefore, we need to be able to draw the distinction between actually releasing ourselves to the laws of the Divine, and simply being misled and assuming that we've surrendered. Being misled equates to "sin" in its root meaning which is "to miss the mark." (Note that I am not referring to "sin" in its popular definition as "to do bad, or wrong, or evil.") But, missing the mark is a serious consideration nonetheless. Thoreau said that most men "...lead lives of quiet desparation." That's missing the mark! It is not good enough to have a quietly desparate, or even a peaceful and benign, life. A neutral existance is not good enough. It is true, as Marcel has stated, "If you are not part of the solution, you're part of the problem."

To find out what the laws of the Divine are and to submit oneself to them, i.e. to literally be at the effect of those laws, however that shows up, is terrifying to most people. When ego confronts this work it doesn't recognize that to surrender to the Will of God is not to be killed, but rather, just to submit to a different dynamic, that's all. Ego is never satisfied unless it is making all the rules, pulling all the strings and controlling every detail, not only in its own case, but in the case of everyone and everything in its field of influence. So, once it realizes that one of the purposes of this Work is to shift the context of itself, it begins to put up barriers and resistances. Ego says, "This is not right. It's dangerous. You are in the wrong place. You better get away. The teacher is crazy. The school is made up of a bunch of babies...."

This fear of submission is not surprising. Free will is not one of the laws of the Divine. Free will is a law of this particular species, human beings. But, humans are just one of many species in relationship to God. The Divine laws aren't responsive to the laws of any given species. Humans can desire free will to survive happily all they want, but if they're in the middle of a hurricane, an earthquake, or a forest fire, the law of free will doesn't mean a damn thing.

The Divine paints a vast picture that doesn't take into consideration every little bump on the canvas. And, that is what we are—the whole earth is just one bump on the canvas, and hopefully that consideration sobers you. It's meant to. Just for a moment, at least!

✝ ✝ ✝

Nature has it's own laws based on the physics of things, and nature is not a respecter of creatures, even though many creatures are respecters of nature. Within the animal kingdom it is a common phenomenon that even weeks before a major storm is coming, birds will start to strengthen their nests, and other animals will start to reinforce their shelters to take precautions against the weather. Man, however, doesn't respect nature. He often builds cities on fault lines and floodplanes, and the results are catastrophic.

The laws of God have to do with transformational energies and evolution. Recognizing these evolutionary laws means recognizing that we as a species are quite expendable. The point is not to preserve human life as we know it, but to fulfill our destiny—to do what a human being can do energetically. Often that is in contrast to the expected social norm. Certainly, what Mahatma Gandhi did was antagonistic to the social norm of the time. The same is true for Albert Schweitzer, and Einstein, and Martin Luther King.

In order for one to submit oneself to the effects of the Divine Process, one must have great flexibility in relationship to the laws of human expectation. In the Old Testament there is a brilliant example of this in the story of Abraham and his son Issac. Abraham is commanded by God to make a sacrifice of his first-born son. He took his son up on the mountain and prepared to kill him. That is certainly antagonistic to the laws of humaness. According to the Old Testament, of course, God was so pleased with Abraham's dedication that He spared the life of the boy. This is probably the foundation for the endings of all the fairy tales that say, "...and they lived happily ever after."

The Laws of the Divine have to do with that which always serves a higher dynamic rather than that which serves the lower dynamic. And conversely, the lower dynamic is always served by the excrement of the higher dynamic. You might say that human beings exist on angel shit! In fact, some human beings *are* angel shit, and that's just the way it is.

We human beings are in an ecological chain. If we function according to our elemental being we will serve the ecological chain. We will keep it functioning properly. If we don't, we will tend to interrupt the natural flow in much the same way as the ecological balance in a pond of still water would be interrupted if someone were to pour toxic waste into it. It is our responsibilty to discover that we are part of an ecological chain, and how best to serve that. For instance, there are many different ways that people protest the damage that nuclear radiation does. Some do it by sabotaging nuclear plants. Others protest in another way which may never directly involve social action, or even thinking about the issue of nuclear energy. But, one way or another, the active presence of nuclear energy on the earth today, whether it is thought about, talked about, or done anything about, cannot be ignored. No matter how unconscious or naive one is, the body is going to be affected by it anyway. The presence of nuclear energy is bigger than your petty interest in it or not.

The Russian mystic, George Gurdjieff, used to say that war was necessary to the earth just like certain cultures of bacteria were necessary to the body. Admittedly, that's a pretty radical statement. He went on to explain that there are certain higher forms of life that could not exist without the emanations produced by human suffering, and that those higher forms of life were necessary to sustain another part of the cycle. So, for instance, when a relationship breaks up, or a child or parent dies, there is some suffering generated which feeds these higher entities, but war is like a feeding frenzy. Personally, I find the agonies of war very offensive, and could build a strong case for the fact that it is only man's neurosis that leads to war and that there is nothing of value from it. On the other hand, I'm open to the possibility that Gurdjieff was right. I'm grateful that my expertise isn't in violence or in making weapons, but rather is in a different domain. Whatever my particular area of expertise is, I do that to the best of my ability and avoid trying to outguess the workings of the Process, or the Laws of God. So, to reiterate once again, the most effective use of our energies as human beings is to serve a higher dynamic.

All things in the universe have a certain polarity and we can call the polarities "male and female," or "positive/negative" as in electricity, or simply "polar opposites" as we do when speaking of magnetization. These opposites can also be called Mother Earth and Father God, although it is important to understand that Father God doesn't mean that God is a man. It means that the earth, or creation, or *Shakti* (in Hindu terminology) expresses the feminine principle, while that which is the Ground of Being, or the essential blueprint out of which all of creation arises, is called Father God because it's the masculine principle. Remember, it has nothing to do with men and women as we understand them.

Human beings can only serve one of those two masters, not both. At least not well. A concert pianist cannot also be a prima ballerina, not because the talent isn't there, simply because the time, energy, focus and dedication involved needs to be given to one thing to do it optimally. One expression is not more useful than the other. The value or purity of either one depends on why you're doing it, not what you are doing, particularly. Incidently, however, if one serves Father God one also serves Mother Earth, because it is out of the Ground of Being that manifestation has arisen. If one serves Mother Earth one doesn't necessarily serve Father God, except incidentally, by virtue of the fact that Mother Earth is a manifestation of that which is the Ground of Being.

Father God is like a pregnant woman—but eternally pregnant. Creation is like a constantly gestating or constantly evolving being. Obviously then, to serve the mother always serves the fetus since the health of the mother, not just physically but psychologically and so on, directly affects the fetus. To serve the fetus, however, may only indirectly serve the mother—in the sense that the mother wants a healthy child. Serving the fetus primarily won't necessarily serve the mother's physical and psychological health.

There are a lot of very good people who are serving Mother Earth in effective, practical and meaninful ways. Stephen Gaskin, for instance, developed a community of people in Tennessee. He went down to Central America to teach people to grow soybeans and to use the land optimally for the production of food. In the roughest, most violent neighborhood in the South Bronx, N.Y., he developed a local ambulance service, with trained medical technicians to handle emergency cases and to take local people to the hospitals. Some of my own students are involved in various kinds of medical programs, hospice work, work with elderly and emotionally disturbed, and that's fine because people need to work and that's good work! But, at the same time, their primary focus is on the work we are doing together, which in my perspective is serving the Ground of Being, rather than directly serving Mother Earth.

I don't throw garbage out of the car, and I don't go around hunting just for the fun of shooting animals, and I don't lead a life that really damages the earth in a visible way. At the same time, I admit that is just my particular aesthetic. It's an eccentricity. My attention is completely focused on transformation of individuals, not the salvation of a certain ecology. The work of serving Father God is about a given individual becoming a literal generator, or a transformer. Typically, however, this kind of work shows up on a very personal level, not on a universal level. The effect at the universal level is highly significant, but the tangibility is invisible at that level. You only know that effect by direct knowledge, not by circumstantial feedback.

Some people have an organic disposition toward serving Father God. Some people have an organic disposition toward serving Mother Earth. For example, one person may be moved toward prayer or contemplation which may isolate them from ordinary social circumstances. For others, any kind of isolation or exclusivity is anathema. Their greatest ecstacy in life may be picking grapes with migrant workers out in the field. Or they may choose to serve Mother Earth by assisting at the birth of a child—laughing and celebrating.

In making a decision about working with one particular teacher, it is helpful to know whether you are moved toward serving Father God or Mother Earth, because most schools of spiritual work, and most teachers, are very clearly defined in terms of where their intention is, or what their work will particularly effect. It is also possible that at some phases of life we are oriented to serve one or the other. Timing is everything.

The second implication of the Law of Sacrifice relates to the definition of the word sacrifice itself, meaning to literally "give up something that was being held or treasured." If someone is very comfortable, economically, he or she can more actively and aggressively pursue self-development, because they don't have to worry about spending all their time obsessed with work just to pay the rent. So, there is a very positive effect of being economically comfortable. On the other hand, if comfort were sacrificed, either for a period of time by choice, or because of a stock market crash or something, the benefit to the being of having to support themselves in a different way would also be extremely valuable to one's spiritual development.

In trips to India that I've made with community members, we could have easily afforded to rent private cars and stay in hotels with hot water, but we chose to live in places that none of us, as comfortable middle-class Americans, would have imagined staying in. There were difficulties that arose from this choice. There were lots of resistances triggered—resistances to insects, or resistances to rats, for example. But, once the difficulties were moved through, there were also significant benefits. This dimension of the Law of Sacrifice is the intentional side. We can decide to experiment within the relative domain and take on tasks that will demand that we sacrifice comfort. (Gurdjieff used the term "conscious suffering." Carlos Castenada talked about taking on a "petty tyrant"— one whose presence around you would be a constant source of irritation, and work. And, all of this, with the right intention, can be valuable.)

There is some safety inherent in this aspect of the Law. If you intentionally take a job with someone you know is a "petty tyrant" in order to make work for yourself, you can always quit the job if it gets too hot. The other side of the Law, the part that has to do with you being "food for something higher"…if and when that Law impresses itself upon you, and you become a sacrifice, there is nothing you can do to stop it.

The expertise I've developed as a teacher is literally handicapped by the willingness of students to be assumed by the Law of Sacrifice (that which says that everything in the universe is food for something higher.) Yet the Influence, that I represent, always knows the strengths and weaknesses of a given individual even when "I" have no idea ("I" meaning my psychology or my practical experience). So, for instance, if someone asks a question, Lee Lozowick could hear the question and feel that the questioner is sincere. But beyond that...? The Influence, however, knows how far the questioner is willing to go even though the question is completely honest.

To reiterate: My ability as a teacher to generate circumstances that serve the Law of Sacrifice is unlimited. At the same time, the practical application or manifestation of unlimited potential is directly limited by the willingness of students to "eat" the food I provide. There may be some significant frustrations in this dynamic, because when students *feel* they're ready, they *feel* they're ready! And their readiness is usually based on an honest observation of at least one element of their consciousness, but not all the rest. Who I work for, however, never makes the mistake of misjudging alignment. Who I work for recognizes every element in every domain and exactly how the alignment is placed, and whether it will work in a particular way.

There is a degree of this work that will always be Mystery. A degree of faith will always be needed. One who works with me must be willing to recognize that I may have my opinions and my idiosyncracies, but the Influence is never wrong. My teaching work is not something I do in between going to movies and sleeping. It's absolute. I have no life, literally I don't have one second's breath outside of my relationship to my students. It's a closed chamber. If I'm not giving people things to do, that is not an arbitrary personal choice. When a teacher has no life outside of his relationship with his students, then the Influence decides those things.

A Dialogue About Surrender

QUESTIONER: I have the feeling that I know enough, more than enough even, about making my life work. Yet, one thing I avoid is to surrender to a person as the bridge to surrender to God. I've gone searching. I've been learning from everything. I practice, but still there's something missing in my life and I don't know exactly what it is, or what holds me back? But I do know that this is the only thing that interests me now.

LEE: That's sensible. You're lucky. What do you think it would cost you to surrender to someone? Practically, what do you think you would have to give up—beauty, friendship, respect, non-runnable mascara?

Q: Last year I had a dream that I had to give up everything which gives strength. I knew that I couldn't go on doing what I was doing for work. But, the issue of security is a big one for me.

LEE: So, would you have to leave your work and do nothing, or would something else show up once you left your work, do you think?

Q: Logic says that something else would come up, but emotionally. . . .

LEE: Do you think you could surrender without trusting that something else would come up?

Q: I think I could, but I don't *do* it. I can imagine that one could, but I'm afraid. And I'm afraid of being lonely.

LEE: Who wouldn't be, after all. I am too. Every day I wake up in the morning and I pull the covers down over my eyes and I say, "Oh shit. Another day!" Really, I do!

Well, if you surrender you'll probably feel lonely, and alone too (which is different). If you surrender you'll probably feel more alone that you've ever felt, because to actually surrender puts you in a very small company. Those who understand surrender are few, and so far between that you would find yourself very much alone. I'm sorry that I can't paint you a rosier picture. That would be an unfortunate trick.

Q: I don't think I like this idea.

LEE: Good. Now we're getting somewhere. Only a sadist would like this idea. Jesus Christ said, "Follow me." He didn't sit down and say, "Ahh, we need to talk about this, you guys. Uhh, you know, I need some help here, and I'd really appreciate it if you would participate." He said, "Follow me. You don't like where I'm going? Tough shit. Follow me."

You can't muscle this process of surrendering, however. This is not something to which you can say, "I know exactly what he's talking about. I want this, and I'm going to do it." Impossible! It takes more than vulnerability. To elicit something real requires a kind of inspiration! If the right combination of elements is present something can happen, but surrender is not something that I can *make* happen, or that you can make happen.

As I hear you talk about surrender you imply that you don't know what it is, but I disagree with that. If you didn't know what it was you wouldn't want it so badly! Your resistance to surrender both obscures your conscious recognition of what it is and explains away the circumstances in which it is possible.

Q: I am afraid of surrendering too much.

LEE: It's impossible to surrender too much. If one feels one has "surrendered too much," it is not surrender but just self-indulgence under one of its more tricky forms. Self-indulgence can show up as arrogance, protection, and a certain kind of independence. But, it can also show up as a kind of pseudo-surrender of subservience, weakness, and a type of "follower-mentality." Only through real surrender do you realize that what you thought was surrender was just strategized. It was just another expression of the whole ego dynamic. But, not to surrender when you have an opportunity, is to just build up stronger armor around your strategy.

Surrender may be associated with great difficulty, hard work, pain. With surrender one comes to feel a sharpened compassion for all beings, so one consequently feels more pain. There's just no way of getting around it. Yet, at the same time, it is never something that one would wish to be different.

Surrendering is not dual. There is no "one" to wish that it could be different. The difficulty with surrender, from the dualistic perspective, is that surrender looks like extinction. Personality, which by it's very nature is dualistic, thinks that to be non-dualistic would mean being wiped out. It thinks that individuality, independence, one's uniqueness, would be wiped out, but really that's not true. Even Swami Nityandanda in India was an extraordinary individualist. Nobody grunted like him! He just sat around around with his big *Shakti* belly and growled at people and grunted once in a while. And he talked a lot, despite what some of his followers like to say. He talked to children, particularly.

If one would just surrender, and stay in that state, one would realize that actually one is *more* of an individual, because all of a sudden you've got real options. Before surrender all of our options are absolutely defined by our survival strategy, and surrender doesn't look like a graceful, pleasant process to ego.

Q: Okay, but how does one start—how does one begin this process of surrender?

LEE: You look at the environment to which you are attracted—for instance, the company and culture of students around a teacher—and you get the feeling sense of whether you think surrender is possible within that environment, regardless of whether you think you can "do" it or not. If it seems that this place holds that potential, you make the choice to engage the environment. You begin to participate in it. You note what effect the environment is having on you over time. Every once in awhile you bring up the consideration of surrender for yourself. This is important. In an environment such as a spiritual school, change tends to happen slowly and consistantly, like the way a child grows. When you see a baby every day you don't see much change. But, after six months or a year it becomes quite obvious. So, question yourself now and again—"What has happened for me?" And if anything has happened then ask yourself, "Is it useful?" Simple. Don't ask, "Useful for what?" Just ask, "Is it valuable?" Then every once in awhile bring up the question of surrender around the teacher so that they don't forget that this is what you really want.

Then you wait, and you continue to work. Many people, in my experience, will ask the same question over and over again for many years before all the right elements are aligned. Then, just one tap is necessary and they have their answer.

My observation about you is that the question of surrender is honest, not just something you've read about or are curious about. You've come to that out of a sense of urgency. But, it also strikes me that you have a lot to protect—that the lifestyle you've chosen for yourself is one in which you have developed an incredibly sophisticated armory. The issue of surrender, in your case, is not one that can be handled quick and easy—like one, two, three. But, one thing is for sure, to really handle that issue would be worth whatever it cost!

Time isn't slowing down. We don't have all the time in the world, despite the fact that "we" don't die when the body goes. It is possible that when this form dies we will forget everything that we've learned while it was alive. We might not, but there's no guarantee either way. Even the chance, then, that we might forget everything should really inspire us to work like hell while we are alive. Man! who wants to do all this over again? Do you know what I mean? Maybe next lifetime you won't show up looking like you do now, one of the beautiful people. Maybe next lifetime you'll be all twisted and deformed, or insane. It's hard enough to do spiritual work as it is now. It's really imperative that we don't waste time. On the other hand, all the things you have done to avoid surrender up till now can be really valuable experiences to have had—talents and gifts that you can use on the other side of it, for instance. People who are good teachers, and I expect you are, always end up maintaining their talent as good teachers. They may just change what they teach.

In my own case, before I began this type of Work, I used to teach Silva Mind Control. I had several thousand students and whenever I held a seminar there would be hundreds of people who would come. When I began this Work that I am doing now, I invited everybody who had previously associated with me to attend a meeting to explain to them how my work had changed. Out of all those thousands of people less than a hundred came. Out of the ones who came, only thirty-five ended up staying. But, at least it was a start. Teaching is teaching, however. It was my job. I just simply got handed a different assignment.

The fact that your question has such urgency now is a sign that it will become a matter of wasting time if you don't act. If this environment, that I represent, is not the one in which it becomes possible to act, I would certainly wish for you to find the right one soon, and I would be more than happy to recommend you for admission wherever you decide to work. If by some bizarre quirk of fate, however, this becomes the environment for you, we'll have some good fights, in between the laughter.

I'm joking and laughing and making fun with you now, but I know what you want and it's a serious affair. Believe me, I take it seriously.

Chapter Ten

ASKING THE RIGHT QUESTION

What the teacher often does is not *answer* a question, but rather help the student to redefine the question until it becomes a workable and vital one. And that process keeps everything on edge. A friend of mine used to teach a form of massage that imbalanced the nervous system, deliberately. His idea was that when we are in balance we're satisfied and won't ask the questions that we have. Imbalance, on the other hand, is like a constant irritant in the sense that it keeps urging us on to find the solution, which means an end of the irritation.

In reality there is only One Question, and if a person comes to that question exactly, the answer is immediately obvious. The question itself doesn't need to be spoken.

When I ask for questions, one of the things that I'm always looking for is the kind of question that I can answer with another question. I want to help you get to the bottom-line question. But that doesn't happen very often. Usually the questions people ask are honest attempts for more information, so generally I just respond in the way that they ask. But, I'm always fishing for something bigger to work with.

You may have a real question, and you many mean it honestly, but if you are not also vulnerable and in a state of irritation about it, my response to you cannot be genuinely helpful. It doesn't pay the teacher to pursue that with the student. The kind of intensity you need to bring to your questions in order to elicit a helpful answer is rare indeed. There must be real disturbance—even a desperation. People who are successful in the ways of the world, however, aren't terribly interested in throwing themselves off balance in order to be vulnerable.

Real questions may have a childish languaging because real questions are a function of attention not just a function of curiosity. If I say to someone, "Good question…" I don't mean that because they really thought it out, and it was so intelligent and articulate, but because there was attention there. So, even if the questioner can't speak a work of English and it has to be translated, I would appreciate that it was a good question before I heard the translation. Even before I open my mouth, I know whether the question is good by how I feel when I hear it. I can also tell if a question is good by how I answer it, or by whether I'm interested, or bored by it. When I'm interested, the answer is always incredible, not always to the questioner himself, but to someone in the space. When I'm bored, however, sometimes I can generate a little passion in the answer, but it's never a "good" answer.

It is very frustrating, sometimes, for people who have been students for a long time, because when new students ask questions, the attention they may get is something the older students may not have received for years. Often new students bring a tremendous innocence and vulnerability into this work. They are like the song… "Fools rush in where angels fear to tread…" Senior students, or mature students, are also fools, but then the transition from just an innocent fool to a conscious fool has its stresses and tensions. Older students have already become suspicious. Often there is a stage in one's practice where one becomes a bit standoffish and a little bit suspicious. It is not that these senior students would leave the school or do anything else (I mean there is nothing else to do), but just that they know the price is so high. New students, however, don't know what they're getting involved with. They don't know the price that this work costs to ego. If they have any resistance at all it is usually not resistance of the heart, but rather a kind of intellectual prejudice, or perhaps just a bad feeling about gurus or something.

You will often see a dramatic difference in how I answer a question, even if the question seems to be very sincere, and very intentional, and very honest. Just because someone is sitting on the edge of the seat, supposedly with so much attention, and acts like he is going to explode if he doesn't get the answer, it doesn't mean there is any real attention there. There might be no attention. The intellect can mimic emotional behavior so well that you actually think you're full of passion when really you're just full of empty, impotent, and romantic illusions.

To some degree the questions you ask should be your way of deciding whether the teacher is just a liar, an opportunist, or whether there's something of real value there. America and Europe both are full of teachers who are just creeps. There's no other way to say it. Complete frauds. But even so, most of them are very intelligent, very clever and they know the parables and sometimes they make a good point. Nonetheless, my advice to you is just keep your clothes on, and don't take your hand off your wallet. And keep those creeps away from your children too.

A teacher's ability to be clever is not a sign of integrity. Anyone who stands up and presents himself or herself as a teacher usually has some intelligence. Instead of looking for cleverness you should be testing my willingness to serve you, or my willingness to take advantage of you; and I'm not going to help you. I mean, I'm not going to make it easy. I want you to have to work a little to test me. I will try to be a little bit sly, and a little bit provocative, and hope that if you have a Real Question, or if you feel something Real, you'll push it, and not just sit back.

A Few Questions

QUESTIONER: Are we equals? What would it take for us to be equal? Can you learn from me as I learn from you?

LEE: Our relationship to one another is like a form of reciprocal feeding. I can provide a certain food for you, and individuals and circumstances provide food for me, food to build on. It's not that I'm "learning" from you, because I can't really learn anything anymore. Playing the flute or painting or cooking—these are just irrelevant elements of life that one picks up as one goes along the path. Really there is only one thing to learn, and that is, what is Truth. Within the realization of Truth there are no distinctions. Everything is known directly and so nothing can be said about it.

QUESTIONER: You speak critically about metaphysics. Why is that?

LEE: I used to do Tarot readings, and I was really hot. But, I got very frustrated because I would do a reading and suggest certain considerations, which would be accurate to the letter, and people would do exactly the opposite of what the reading recommended. They would come back to me and say, "You didn't tell me that." Then we started putting the readings on tape, but they would lose the tapes.

Finally, I stopped doing Tarot readings. It drove me crazy that people would literally hear the opposite of what I was saying. I would speak very clearly, very exactly, and they would sit and look at me and nod, "I understand..." Somehow when you tell people about the future it seems very real to them. Then the future happens, and all of a sudden it isn't the future they thought they were seeing when they heard about it six months before.

I used to do astrology charts too, so when I criticize metaphysics I know what I'm talking about. It's not that the laws and principles of metaphysics are not true. Quite the contrary. They are true. Yet the tendency of human beings to use metaphysical truths to excuse their own despicable behavior is too common for my liking. I stopped doing astrology readings because of people's worship of it, and then their refusal to take seriously the indications. It was just too frustrating. Then too there was the almost universal willingness of people who give readings to manipulate power for their own neurotic reasons. You know how impressionable people are when they believe in something. The astrologer goes, "Hmmh...." The person says, "What?" The astrologer says, "Oh, oh nothing...." That bit of interaction could influence someone beyond anything that the astrologer says from then on. The whole mood of people in the helping professions to see the dark side of a situation instead of the bright side of a situation is really a very serious consideration.

QUESTIONER: Isn't there that same danger in the way people relate to you as a teacher?

LEE: Obviously, the implications of that in my job are also extreme. As a teacher what I'm attempting to teach is as scientific as astrology, and astrology is very scientific. It's not some silly imagination. Yet it doesn't have the tangible foundation—the mathematics, for instance—that astrology does. The scientific basis of the work that I do deals with elements that we are not trained to recognize. The educational system that most of us have been trained in doesn't handle these subject matters. It is very important when people are encouraged to devote themselves to this work and to trust my judgement as a teacher that they recognize the tendency toward being easily hurt or easily influenced, which is a result of giving one's trust. During our time together then, you should get a sense of whether I will take advantage of your tendency to be easily influenced, or whether I will be responsible for the effects of that, guarding against it in every possible way.

QUESTIONER: I have no idea why I'm here, really, but I do know that if you have a connection to God then I can't afford not to be here.

LEE: Well, I hope that you find that out before the weekend is over. I could use some confidence. Sooner or later that should be everybody's response—that if, in fact, I have some genuine connection to God, you can't afford to look the other way. I don't mind being tested, challenged, questioned in this regard. . .but please no crosses and nails. To take a teacher is a very big step and you shouldn't engage that process lightly. Form is often deceiving, so we have the old adage, "Don't judge a book by its cover." What you need to discover is a feeling sense of "no dissonance." To put it positively, what you need to find is a real sense of resonance to the teacher's being, regardless of language, lifestyle, theatrics, and so on. In my own case, when I'm at home, I don't pick up all my clothes, I don't fold all the laundry properly and all that. I am, however, completely responsible to students, and that needs to be observed and recognized. By nature I'm relatively lazy. I don't exercise much, and I'd rather sit home and read a book than get up and go look at churches and architecture and museums and all those wonderful things. But, I am never lazy when it comes to work with my students. Those kinds of distinctions and discriminations need to be made as a form of verifying the teacher's literal responsibility to you. "I" don't need to be trusted, what I represent is what needs to be trusted, and you need to get a feeling sense of what that is.

Q: But didn't you say earlier that it is you who is teaching, so we have to trust you?

LEE: No. The distinction is that when I say "me" I mean what my presence in this room generates. I don't mean this man who is sitting in front of you. The man is often a *"sheisekopf."*

QUESTIONER: I observed you in a public talk the other night when people were yelling at you and walking out, and it seemed like you were thrown off center by what happened. Is that true?

LEE: I was thrilled with the evening, and found the particular dynamic there was more experimental than what we are doing here, and I like that. Often, in experimental circumstances, I can be thrown off from a certain momentum that I've been building, or I can be confused in particular ways. One of the essential principles of this work is that if you surrender to what I call Divine Influence, or the Will of God, who you are (your energy, your personality inclusively) gets used for that process. That doesn't always mean that you're going to be in control of things. Sometimes it means just the opposite. You will be out of control, because that's the dynamic that optimizes the particular experiment.

When I'm thrown off center, the mind's usual stream of consciousness arises about, "You're losing it. Get back in control." Yet, at the same time there's a recognition that to be in control is not the point. To be surrendered to the Will of God is the point. If, in fact, that is true for me, nothing can happen to me to lessen my Work or to discolor or poison the space I'm in. It can't. It's impossible. If, on the other hand, that is just my illusion, then that will get shown to me very clearly. Circumstances will conspire to effectively undermine or destroy that which I think I'm attempting to do.

There is a saying in Werner Erhard's teaching which is: "Reality is hard and persistent and will knock you on your ass every time." The point of this work is not that you can transcend reality, because reality is a lawful process and we're in it. If this work is true of you, when you get knocked on your ass, which you will because "reality is hard and persistent and...knock(s) you on your ass every time"—you won't mind it because you'll recognize that it's a function of this work. It's a lawful process.

But, if this work is not true of you and you get knocked on your ass, you're not going to like it one bit. You're going to fight it tooth and nail, right down to the nail, even though reality is going to knock you on your ass every time whether you fight it or not.

Control is not the point. The point is to be what is wanted and needed, wherever and whenever. That is a matter of feeding what the space needs, not superimposing on the space what you would like, or how you would like to define it. The particular *actions* are not the point so much as the *context* in which the actions are held or performed.

There was once a Zen teacher named was Ikku. His monastery was located right across the street from a whorehouse. Ikku would sit in meditation and when he was done sitting he would get up in his robes and go across the street to the whorehouse and entertain some women. He would drink, and write poetry to them, and read to them, and teach them about Zen. And they would then do their poetry on him. Yet, I don't think he or anyone else would say that every customer who came to the whorehouse was a Zen master. The act was the same. The difference was context. So, like that.

QUESTIONER: I know that the Bauls are noted for their use of sexual energy. Can you give initiation in this use?"

LEE: The price that I want people to pay for specific instruction in the transformation of sexual energy is that they be involved in a committed, working relationship for at least a couple of years. Commitment means that you are with one person and, like the traditional vows, you plan to be with that person forever, no matter what.

Commitment means that the mood of your relationship to your mate is much the same mood as one's relationship to parents, or to one's children in the sense that you never question that your children are your children, or your parents are your parents. Typically, relationships with mates tend to be: "If it doesn't work, I'll find another sex partner." Our relationship to our children, on the other hand, is never, "If you don't get 'A's in school I'll find another child," even though we might say that once in a while, because children can be pretty maddening.

Given the nature of the wanderlust of Western man or woman, it's probably obvious that few people have that kind of relationship, in or out of community. When someone does, the form of instruction I give begins with the subtleties of disposition, not with what the genitals do mechanically.

Q: What do you mean by 'disposition'?

LEE: The way one needs to be within the particular relationship, or the way one feels about the particular relationship, rather than what one actually does with it.

QUESTIONER: What is the advantage of a long-term relationship for transforming sexuality?

LEE: The more energy we have at our disposal, the more actively we can serve, in a physical way. The wastefulness of the way sex is used typically involves so much energy—energy that is then unavailable to the process of worship, adoration, prayer.

Prayer is not a static...not a cool process. It's hot, and active, and energetic, like the mad wanderer in India who goes around singing, and dancing and praising God. In many native cultures, the way one gets to be the tribal shaman is not by the rational process of study, but by going mad. The madness is a function of being thrust into the underworld and having to make friends with that which the underworld is.

Now, one can deal with the upperworld without much energy, because in the upperworld one is transported, one is carried. One doesn't climb the mystical ladder of ascent, rather one is drawn up. But, to deal with the underworld, which is one of the three worlds of the human kingdom, that takes energy—power.

It takes power to deal directly with fear, with conflict, with anger, with violence, with illness, which are all underworld elements. To use an example, take the myth of Amor and Psyche. Psyche fell in love with Amor and it was required that she never look at him. Eventually, though, she did look at his face and was cursed—banned to the underworld from which she eventually found her way back to her lover. That release required an almost superhuman amount of energy. When a Shaman is required to heal, the Shaman goes into the underworld, deals with the spirits of the disease, and then returns. Without a tremendous reservoir of energy, one who was thrust into the underworld wouldn't be able to find the upperworld again. But, with energy, even without sophistication, just with enough energy, one could find the way out.

One of the most passionate confessions of how sexual energy relates to spiritual work is found in the diary of Vaslev Nijinsky, the dancer. Now Nijinsky didn't have a broad matrix in which to apply the energy that he was at the effect of, and so he went mad.

Even though he was a raving maniac throughout most of his life, there were moments of breathtaking clarity in between his madness. When he was clear he was really clear, like any master—like Jesus, or Buddha. He really *knew*. Actually, we should probably call him a lunatic rather than a maniac because he also recognized a very significant relationship to energy dynamics. Lunatic, as you know, has to do with the moon, with energy dynamics that are much too subtle for most people to appreciate.

QUESTIONER: In which way are you transforming this sexual energy? Are you taking something away, adding something, or just making gold. . .or magic?

LEE: Making gold out of metal. We aren't adding anything, although some of the men in the community wish we could add an inch or two.

Technically, a lot of the tantric literature that is readily available deals with conservation of orgasm and so on. It covers these superficial elements. Orgasm requires a tremendous expenditure of energy. Most men, I have found, feel better when the woman they are having sex with is screaming and thrashing and moaning and weeping. A big part of man's relationship to transformative energy within relationship has to do not just with the physiological, but with his psychological needs in relation to women. Both men and women need to learn to read what's in the eyes, and what's in the aura, beyond just what the body is craving or animating.

To conserve the energy of orgasm is a basic principle. Part of the training in transformation of sexual energy is in having the body learn what to do with all the energy once it is contained. That is a lot of energy, and people get wired and tense with it pretty easily. First of all, it is important to understand that conservation of orgasm is not equated with elimination of orgasm. Secondly, just to conserve orgasm and then to hyperventilate a couple of times a week, or to do triathalons once a week, isn't exactly the process I'm recommending either.

Q: How does the body learn to do that?

LEE: The *body* learns. The mind doesn't learn. That is a very, very, very important distinction. To use an example. There is a Canadian woman in this school who was a concert pianist. At eight years of age she was touring Canada as a child prodigy. At fourteen she was in Vienna training with the top piano teacher in that city. Yet she gave up touring to pursue work with spiritual teachers. When she came to my school she stopped playing the piano for the first five or six years. Then one day she rented a piano and just started playing again. She said that her playing was better after five years of no practice than it was when she was touring and practicing for eight hours a day.

During those first years when she was in the school her body was learning below her level of observation. She just worked hard and did her spiritual practices to the best of her ability, and struggled intensely with her emotions. That whole process was training her body in ways that the body recognized, but the mind couldn't make any sense of it whatsoever.

The body will know when it is given certain benediction. The mind, the intellect, may or may not know. Definitions have their value. Intellectualism has its value, yet in a lot of areas it is not necessary even though it is enjoyable and appreciable. Timing is most crucial, and that is where I come in. The proper timing in this kind of work is almost more important than knowledge.

My relationship to the Divine is to be surrendered to that which seeks manifestation as the Will of God. I have found myself having the unconscious ability to provide people with work circumstances which will train their bodies, absolutely, in ways that nothing else can. I am not unintelligent, and at the same time, there are many aspects of this process that I don't understand intellectually at all. That doesn't matter. I can feel the rightness of what I can provide for people, and I can also feel the dissonance of not providing the exactly correct circumstance for any given individual.

My work as a teacher is not done based on efforts of will. The work I provide for people, which is what trains the body, is based on an unconscious response to the ultimate need of the circumstance. The Divine Process works through me. I'm just a conduit for that benediction.

QUESTIONER: When one has a free moment... a moment in which one is operating without the usual mechanical functioning...does that mean that one is happy in that moment?

LEE: Good question. Let me try to define happiness.

To ego, happiness is being in control. For instance, we have desire and we succeed in getting the things we desire, so we are happy. That *might* be real happiness—that is a philosophical point. Yet, one thing is for sure, that type of happiness is always temporary because it relies completely on the satisfaction of certain desires or on the ability to control and manipulate the environment and our circumstance.

Desires are based on insecurity. We always feel we are somehow incomplete without what it is we desire. When we do get it, we are happy. We are no longer insecure. In a free moment, however, the issue of incompleteness or insecurity is irrelevant. These states do not exist in the domain of true freedom. In a free moment we simply are complete. We do not question it. That is happiness. In form we may be laughing, or we may be weeping. It doesn't matter. We're happy. (And I don't think you could find a truly compassionate man or woman who wasn't happy.)

To resolve the issue that all life is suffering should be consuming your whole life, attention and energy. There is a very delicate balance between that obsession and the common tendency to righteousness and rigid dedication to principle. The resolve that happens with the true understanding that "all life is suffering" automatically provokes the realization of happiness—joy, communion and delight. It actually transforms one from an "animal" into an essentially attractive human being. . .one who is transcendent, who literally floats through life, without defining or restricting the form that life takes. Like Henry Miller (who is probably my single, greatest spiritual hero), many artists have fit that description. They are full of life, passionate, and yet they still appear to be seriously tortured individuals. It doesn't matter. They have realized that all life is suffering and that, coincident with that reality, there is also joy, ecstasy and delight. There is beauty. There is the sacred. There is food, sex, money. All of it!

QUESTIONER: How would I realize that a transformation process had taken place in me?

LEE: My ex-wife was a nurse in a hospital, and one day she came home and told me that an amazing thing had happened. A thirty-year-old woman came into the hospital complaining of stomach pains, and when they got her up on the table, she gave birth. When she saw the baby, she looked at the doctor in all innocence and said, "Where did this come from? How did this happen?" And no amount of explaining seemed to satisfy her.

Now, that is an exceptional case. Most people, when they're pregnant, they know it. Women don't usually ask, "How will I know if I'm pregnant?" The answer to that is, "You just know!" And the same applies to the question about realizing transformation. The answer is, "Well, you'll just know." If you have a certain sense of honesty about your own process, when transformation is evident there will be no questions about the process.

QUESTIONER: I have heard it said that the "Spiritual Heart" of the earth is moving from the East to the West. Do you agree with that, and what would be the implications of such a shift?

LEE: The Spiritual Heart of the world moves around the earth from time to time. Now, despite the great power of the Hopis, the Navajos and other Native American cultures, and the profoundly advanced civilizations like the Mayans, Aztecs and Incas, the actual Heart of spirituality on the earth has not been in the West yet. (It may have been here before we read about it historically, however.) The Spiritual Heart of the earth has been in the East, and only now is it moving to the West. A lot of the upheaval that our world is experiencing is a result of this movement.

Before the Spiritual Heart actually becomes established and radiating in the West, the West needs to be purified for that purpose. Often, in many physical healings, the actual turning point of the healing is preceded by what is called the "healing crisis." That is when the illness gets much worse before it gets better. That's happening now. The earth is having a crisis, and we're just touching the surface of that crisis. We haven't seen the force or heat of it yet. Of course, all the metaphysical and spiritual predictions say that we will see the heat of it in our lifetime, and those who are ready will survive, while those who aren't ready won't. It's very simple.

Survival won't be dictated by who has the most guns and who has the strongest fort. It's very different. Survival will be dictated by who has the most flexible being…who has the greatest ease of response to unexpected circumstances…who can "give in so as to conquer." One of the most important aspects of the martial art form known as *Aikido* is not to confront force with force, but to use force to essentially turn around what's going on. When someone attempts to attack or be forceful in a circumstance, the *Aikido* practitioner, or the *Judo* practitioner, simply moves out of the way, not necessarily physically, but energetically. If you as an individual try to meet force with force…. You're going to stand in front of an earthquake and meet that? You're going to stand in front of a tidal wave or a hurricane and meet that? Don't be ridiculous. You can stand at the lip of a volcano and pray all you want, say every mantra you know, and you are still going to be covered with lava. Crisped!

There is a profound attempt to use force to sustain life and to avoid death. It's a terrifying experience to feel helpless. This issue of force is a vital one to us as a way of recognizing the dynamic that we attempt to work with in life instead of the dynamic we should be employing—that of submission.

Q: How does one learn this process?

LEE: It is obvious that one needs a tremendous amount of expertise to "give in so as to conquer," otherwise one gives in and *gets* conquered.

I once studied with a *Judo* master who would let us try to practice "giving in so as to conquer…," but we never conquered, even though he would occasionally let us think that we had. Invariably we'd still find ourselves on the ground, with him standing over us. You can't just let go and expect that nothing will happen. You could get robbed!

A lot of what a spiritual school does is train people to have the expertise of surrender. We have learned that life is hard and that it pushes us around and that we had damn well better stand on our own two feet and take care of ourselves. That disposition doesn't surrender easily. It requires a tremendous amount of training, and time, and attention, and so on. People can talk about the principle of "giving in so as to conquer" in *Judo* all they want, but if they don't learn the throws, the stances, and how to use their energy, nothing will ever happen. They'll never learn.

Q: Are you suggesting that we just submit to everything? What about the use of violence?

LEE: The *Bhagavad Gita* is a profound source of wisdom in this case. It is, as some of you may know, the part of the traditional Hindu scripture that is a discussion between Krishna, who's considered one of the great Hindu gods, and one of his students, a man named Arjuna. Essentially, the student is a warrior. One day, Arjuna learns that his cousins, his uncles, and others of his family will be on the opposing side in a battle, and he doesn't want to fight. He wants to somehow solve the problem without fighting, without violence. Well, to make an really extraordinary scripture very short and concise (and I would recommend that everybody read the *Bhagavad Gita* if you haven't), Krishna says to Arjuna: "You have no other choice but to fight because that is your destiny. You *do* have a choice about your attitude. If you fight under the illusion that you're killing someone, and that the fight will make a difference universally, then you are already conquered before you even strike a blow. But, if you recognize who it is that gets killed…if you question, 'Is there such a thing as death?' or 'What is changed actually?'…and you fight simply because it's your destiny, not because it means anything, then you've given in and conquered already."

If you need to defend your home, you defend your home. The principle of "giving in so as to conquer" is not something that we can effectively generate in an entire culture in a lifetime. But, you defend your home without prejudice, without vindictiveness, and without the mood of vengeance. If you have to defend, you defend simply because that's the way you protect your family and your culture. You don't defend because you hate the enemy.

There are many young Jews who have never been out of the U.S. and had nothing to do with the Second World War. They had no family killed, even. Yet, they still blame Germans of your age for what happened forty or fifty years ago. That attitude itself is the essential basis of all violence—a violence that only breeds more violence.

QUESTIONER: I have occasionally had the experience of being in the mood of surrender. My question is, how do I keep this or hold it?

LEE: When you are in that state, remember, if you can, that your ability to sustain that state has to do with your organic matrix, not with what your mind or your ego wants to do. If you're in that state, you question yourself, "What would help build that matrix?" You then act upon the answer to that question. You either have to remember to use the question yourself, or you need to rely on the help of other members of the body-of-work that you are doing to help generate the question for you.

In an enlightened or surrendered mood, a question of "could this experience go away?" would never arise. In that mood there is also the instinctual knowledge that, *"Enlightenment is the knowledge that all experience is transitory, including enlightenment."* [This is one of the fundamental principles of Lee's teaching. Editor.] One knows that this state or experience will pass, yes, and so what? It doesn't mean anything, because, *"Enlightenment is the knowledge that all experience is transitory including enlightenment."*

The other important point to realize is that with this surrendered mood or state it should not be assumed that now you have no more work to do. The disposition of no-resistance, or enlightenment, is identical to the disposition of no-choice about working. When that free space of nonresistance tends to fade, it is obvious that one should just keep on working. Doubt may come in, but what stays is no question about working, even though the ease and gracefulness leave.

QUESTIONER: How can you do the work you say you do with students if you are in the U.S. and the student is in Germany, for instance?

LEE: My attention is given to students when they make themselves noticeable.

There are three ways for students to make themselves noticeable. One is the grossest way, which is just to write and to keep up a kind of consistent objective communication. And, under those circumstances distance means nothing. So, if I get a letter from someone every month, my attention is always there.

The second way is for the student to seriously engage specific recommendations for practice that are a function of this school. One can do that in one of two ways. The first is simply mechanically—just like a formula. So, for instance, the teaching has touched you and you want it, and to get it you do the conditions. You don't do the conditions because you *feel* to do them, but like a business. When one practices that way, essentially they're buying my attention, which is better than not having it. The other way you can practice is because you feel a resonance. That won't make the practices easy, necessarily. The resonance is not to the practices themselves, but to the essential vision of the teacher. The third way that one can get my attention is by feeling a longing for that which I represent. Any of these three ways elicits my attention.

When one feels a longing for that which I represent, the typical progression of that dynamic is this: First, one tends to feel that he or she has got to have the physical teacher's personal attention.

145

It's almost like a love affair, and can exhibit all the emotional dynamics of a love affair. That initial response tends to move into a recognition that the teacher stands in two worlds and acts as a kind of gateway between the worlds. That can be a difficult period, because by that time the student is deeply bonded to the teacher and yet feels that the teacher is almost lying or cheating, or somehow hiding this important secret. Some students become very abusive at that stage, which is certainly not one of the job benefits of *my* work. Fortunately for everybody, some move through the abusive period very quickly. The third stage is when the student sees the teacher for exactly what he or she is, without confusion, and without fuzziness. (And there's no need to say *what* that is because it sounds self-serving and egotistical when I say it. If you were to say it now it would just smell like cheap perfume and sound like horrible poetry.)

I hope you have that longing aspect. But, if you don't, what can you do? Actually, it is a tremendously feminine response, and a lot of men have that response, but it is very threatening. A lot of men have have spent their whole lives trying to be MEN! Warriors! Heroic, strong, untouchable. Most men "feel" with their heads, and if this work touches them they begin to "think" with their hearts; that is terrifying for some of them. (Almost all therapy tries to develop "thinking" with the emotions. We tend to assume that that is the same as thinking with the *heart* because there is so much expression. But it is not.)

These principles apply to when I'm right here in the same room, as well. Your attention on me in turn elicits my attention on you. But, attention is a technical word. Just because someone looks at me and thinks about me doesn't mean their attention is one me. In America there are people who have been associated with this school for years who haven't elicited my attention yet, even though I know their names and this, that and the other thing about them.

So, my attention is returned in several ways. If my attention is elicited, the Work will continue building momentum. It will move.

It's interesting that the human intellectual domain mimics emotions and feelings so consistently and so well that almost everything we *think* is feeling and emotion, is really just the mind. On the other hand, attention is actually an emotional expression, but it looks intellectual, because when we're paying attention we tend to look like we're concentrating, like we're really intent. The head gets hot, and the mind works, so we think it's intellectual, but it's not at all. Attention has nothing to do with the intellect. And something else which may surprise you, especially if you've been studying work, like the Gurdjieffian material, that articulates distinctions between the three centers, is that *intention* is physical, not emotional or intellectual! This is information you could work on for years, literally just these two statements.

Many people who have never met me, yet who have read one of my books, have had dreams of me. Others have had incredible mystical experiences in their meditation, or in their lives, but none of that has elicited my attention.

When I say "my" I don't mean who you think you're seeing sitting in front of the room. I mean everything that includes *what I represent*—the Work I do spiritually and all of that.

Philosophically, everybody can say "God and I are not separate. I am integrated in the universe and I am one of the cells in the body of God." And philosophically that's true. But, most people that can say that have no resume. They, essentially, have never proved it and couldn't if their lives depended on it.

I have a resume as thick as an encyclopedia! In one sense we're all equal and there's no difference. I've just seen a movie you haven't seen, that's all, and I'm just filling you in on the plot. In another way we are very different. So, just because someone feels a connection to me doesn't meant that they're attracting my attention.

We have mentioned before the story of Orage, one of Gurdjieff's students, who himself had a large following in New York. Many of Orage's students had dreams of Gurdjieff and felt a real, personal connection to him, but almost none of them had ever seen Gurdjieff in person. They felt that they had Gurdjieff's attention (although they probably wouldn't have spoken of it in that way) because of the way they felt about him. At the first meeting that Gurdjieff had with them when he came to America, he gave a very critical talk about their lack of accurate practice and this threw the whole group into a total revolution. Most of those people never took Gurdjieff as their teacher since one of the things he demanded of students was that they attract his attention. Most of these people were not willing to pay the price required to attract his attention.

Phenomena occurring in someone's life that one attributes to a teacher is not indicative of the teacher's attention on that person. It's indicative of the person's fascination with altered states of consciousness.

Q: Can you explain a little more about the "three centers?"

LEE: The intellectual center is loosely associated with the thinking mind and the upper domains of the body. The emotional center, sometimes called the feeling center, is associated basically with the heart, the heart chakra. But again, loosely associated. And the moving center, which is also sometimes called the vital, is associated with what they call in Japanese, the *Hara*. The vital is in the same location as where the *chi* resides in the body. That is what animates us.

QUESTIONER: How does your attention show up in people's lives?

LEE: My attention animates itself in people's lives in several ways. First, through a direct personal response—usually I write back when people write to me from Europe because I don't have that many students there. But, I rarely initiate communication with someone.

How my attention shows up is also just like the Work—i.e. it shows up subtly. It can show up in dreams, but then many people have dreams of me that are not the result of my attention but rather the result of their own imagination.

My attention can animate itself in people's lives by certain clear insights or understandings they have never had before. But then, that can happen from other catalysts too—so that also is a somewhat subtle dynamic. The other way it tends to show up is in a type of internal transformation that is not only not subtle, but so obvious and profound that often people attempt to make it more subtle than any of the subtle influences.

My physical presence with my students who only see me rarely acts to give feedback and refine the elements of my attention that have shown up during my absence. For instance, when T. first connected with the school he came to America right away for several months to live on the Ashram. He worked. He paid attention. Then, he returned to Germany and it was nine months before I saw him again. But, the minute I saw him it was obvious that he looked entirely different. Still it wasn't time for feedback. We spent time together, and traveled around together, but I gave no feedback. This year, however, after not seeing him for eight or nine months, I saw that the work he had done in my absence could use a little refining, so I gave him some feedback, finally.

I send audio tapes of my talks to people who are not physically close. The interesting thing that happens for many, especially those who elicit my attention, is that the tape they receive will contain exactly what they need to hear at the moment. They report that it's almost like the tape has got their name on it, and it's not only because I talk about everything under the sun on every tape.

So, feedback is given when feedback is needed. The sensitive or delicate part of that is that often we think we are ready for feedback when we're really not. Only time and experience gives us the kind of patience to realize that we get what we need when we need it. But, it doesn't always stop the questions, which is fine.

QUESTIONER: How can one be at least a little bit sure that you are putting your attention on him?

LEE: I can only answer that by suggesting that you try it. Then when I come back next year and somebody else asks that question, I point to you as an example.

QUESTIONER: I am suspicious about my longing for God. When I start a relationship with a man I get it all mixed up with my longing for God, feeling that the object of my love is inaccessible. Over the years I have come to believe that I have lost God, in a sense, because God hasn't fulfilled my prayers. He didn't give me what I wanted and intensely longed for.

LEE: First of all, I think that what you describe is a very common experience that many people have. It is certainly not unusual. Things being what they are (our training, our education, even the elements of our bodies) we human beings are encouraged in our misunderstandings, encouraged in a lack of proper distinction-making. We are typically trained, by implication, to believe that God is somewhere else, and if we pray for things we'll get whatever we pray for as long as we pray in the right way.

Q: Doesn't Jesus say, "Knock and door the will be opened?"

LEE: Yes. I will get to that.

One of mankind's answers to suffering is the concept of salvation. To a five-year-old, salvation is a new rocking horse. To a fifteen-year-old, salvation is a young man or a young woman. To a thirty-year-old, salvation is healthy children, or a working relationship. To a sixty-year-old salvation is just health…just no sickness. And, loss of faith is very common because people misunderstand the Divine process. To most people, God is just an element of all of this instead of the essential process of it all.

To respond to your question then, the first element is not to feel that you failed when you were a child, but to recognize that you didn't fail. You simply weren't praying. Real prayer is only adoration. It is never about asking for something. (We do want something, however. It is normal to think, "Why shouldn't we get it?") Jesus said, "Knock and the door shall be opened unto you," but what did he mean by knock, and what did he mean by the door being opened unto you? I would suggest that adoration is knocking, and when you adore all the doors are open to you—door of ecstasy, doors of understanding, doors of clarity, doors of service, and so on.

A second element in your question, is this: one cannot really know God without knowing man. And to know man is not to expect from a human relationship what you would expect from the ultimate purity of the Divine Process. To know man is to recognize, without confusion and doubt, that men and women have hopes, and dreams, and pains, and fears. We are human. In a relationship we need to be willing to give, and we also expect to receive in some degree. To know God is to enable those expectations to be healthy and essentially benign.

To say that once someone becomes the object of your love they become unattainable is just a matter of idealism, not reality. To cease to have this idealism, however, is not to become sober and pessimistic all the time. It is rather to find delight in the ordinary. A relationship that cannot find delight in the ordinary is doomed to failure. A relationship that can't find delight in the ordinary leads to more trips, more fancy meals, more movies, more entertainment, wilder sex...more, more, more, more...until finally it just dies from being overwhelmed by too much stuff.

I came to the conclusion in a moment of dark observation that the entire human race is a function of various degrees of sickness. Yet, God gets served in the midst of who you are and what you're becoming as a human being, not from standing outside of your humanness. Transformation happens in activity...through a process, not in a static state. That process takes place in the midst of our struggles, our neuroses, our fears, our joys, our passions—all together.

Afterword

MEETING MY MASTER

I visited Yogi Ramsuratkumar, my Master and spiritual Father, for the first time in 1976. His Name had been give to me by Hilda Charlton, a wonderful teacher (and one of my early mentors) in New York City.

That first visit was extraordinary. Yogi Ramsuratkumar showered me with attention, affection, and acknowledgement. I was "bitten."

In 1979 I returned to Him for the second time, and again the overwhelming reception was repeated. By 1981 I had decided that He was my Master and began to write Him devotional poetry, of a sort.

I traveled to India again in 1986, this time with twenty-one students and children (who I don't consider students even if they've been born into the school, so to speak). Triumphantly returning to "my Teacher," I was ready to show Him off to my understandably eager travelling companions. Instead, I was in for a big surprise—

153

of the shocking variety. He didn't recognize me, receive me or acknowledge me. In fact, He definitively and unequivocally sent me away with the admonition not to come back.

The details of my "return to grace" make a long, fascinating (even if I do say so myself) and spiritually useful tale which I won't relate here. Suffice it to say that I persisted in my devotional approach to Him, committed myself with Faith and Constancy to His Work, and eventually was welcomed home. (As He has said to Indian devotees, India and His Company had truly been my home many times before.)

In 1987 I was invited to participate (as honored guest speaker, as it turned out, much to my surprise—this time of the delightful variety) in a Jayanthi Celebration for Him in Nagercoil, Kanya Kumari district, in Southern India. He would not be present, but T. Ponkamaraj, an ardent devotee and great lover of Yogi Ramsuratkumar—a man who has since become a beloved friend and *guru bhai* (guru brother)—would be our host. I gratefully accepted the invitation.

A fine party it was too!

I had planned to visit Yogi Ramsuratkumar for two days at the end of this two-and-a-half-week trip, hoping for (but not counting on) some recognition from Him of acceptance as a *chela* or disciple. I was not disappointed. His welcome was beyond anything I had imagined.

Since then, in yearly visits to His home and Ashram in Tiruvannamalai, my relationship to my Father has deepened ongoingly, and His effusive support for our relationship has been evident beyond any possible subtleties. Where this will all lead, only He knows. But, in any case, it is an adventure of proportions that are unthinkable and too profound for language. (Do I sound self-important here? Yes, I believe so. Well, I never said I was humble. Surely the text of this book must have conveyed that.)

My life as a devotee is as rich and deep as my life as a Teacher and guide. Arrogant I may be, but schizophrenic I am not. I lay all the ostensible accomplishments of my life and Work at His Feet. It is all His Benediction. I am nothing without Him.

All praise be His. Jaya Yogi Ramsuratkumar Maharaj. Jaya Bhagawan Yogi Ramsuratkumar.

lee lozowick
Prescott, AZ
July 1995

SRI YOGI RAMSURATKUMAR[1]

God realization manifests in many different forms, from the miraculous or mystical to the ordinary. The sometimes paradoxical appearance of the realized one varies according to God's Will. For some, the form through which awakening manifests is clearly defined and laid out before the aspirant, "This is my teaching. This is the path taken by me to achieve realization and this I pass on to you." For others, the manifestation of God realization is subtle, crazy-wise, or even completely obscure or unknown. There are those who are sometimes called "hidden" Masters, whose work is so absolutely focused on the transformation of the whole of mankind—and into dimensions beyond—that very little of the Masters' attention is placed on individual realization. The work of these Masters is mysterious, their ways known only to the Divine, while they communicate to devotees and the world at large through their inexplicable and enigmatic actions.

---

1 This biography is taken from: *Facets of the Diamond: The Wisdom of India.* Prescott, AZ: Hohm Press, 1994, pp. 31-35.

Yogi Ramsuratkumar is such a God realized Master. The majority of his years in Tiruvannamalai, India—where he lives today—have been spent in solitude as the necessary medium for his unique spiritual work. Clothed in unwashed rags, forever collecting and carrying what would appear to be useless scraps of paper and other refuse and living in garbage heaps, he wandered as a beggar throughout the city for many years as if busily ordering an unseen reality, placing the subtle structure of the universe just so in order to effect God's desired ends. Few discourses on the *dharma* were given, nor extravagant displays of supernatural powers; rather the seeker was enveloped in his spontaneous delight in the Divine, his laughter, and his childlike, playful nature. His eyes sparkling with laughter, he declared over and over again to any and all who listened that all of life, everything, was his Father in Heaven. For Yogi Ramsuratkumar, nothing exists but the Supreme God. It was this childlike delight and play and overflowing love of God that earned Yogi Ramsuratkumar the affectionate title "The Godchild of Tiruvannamalai" from his growing numbers of devotees.

Yogi Ramsuratkumar was born on December 1, 1918, growing up on the holy river Ganges in a remote village just outside the city of Kashi (Varanasi). From the earliest age he was attracted to and inspired by the holy men and *sadhus* who passed through the sacred city, often inviting them home to receive offerings of food. He listened intently to the sweet sound of the river, and developed friendships with those who shared the same desire to know truth. One day in 1947 while speaking with a *sadhu* friend, he told of his deep desire to seek spiritual guidance from a true master and mentioned his interest in the great sage of Pondicherry in Southern India — Sri Aurobindo. The *sadhu* was enthusiastic and added that he should also visit another great Master who lived in the south named Ramana Maharshi. With these two destinations in mind, he began his journey.

The Sri Aurobindo ashram provided a rich source of inspiration for Ramsurat, and he spent his time deep in study of Aurobindo's spiritual and social principles: the idea of the supramental, the importance of the stability and unity of Mother India, and the possibility of the Divine being manifest in physical matter. Since Aurobindo himself was often in seclusion at this late point in his life, Ramsurat asked if there were another sage whose company he might join. A devotee in Pondicherry suggested Ramana Maharshi and Ramsurat immediately remembered his *sadhu* friend's advice and left for Tiruvannamalai.

After staying with Ramana Maharshi and receiving his blessing for three days, someone showed Ramsurat a clipping describing yet a third realized sage in Kerala, and taking this as an omen, he commenced to travel there. The third sage was Swami Papa Ramdas. Ramsurat did not feel the strong connection with Ramdas on this first visit that he had felt with both Sri Aurobindo and Ramana Maharshi. He described himself as having a reaction to the way Papa seemed to be treated like a king, and he immediately left Ramdas to travel back north.

After traveling and wandering for some time he journeyed back south to once again visit the two spiritual giants who had influenced him in 1947. This time he grew restless at the Aurobindo ashram and so went immediately to Tiruvannamalai, where he spent two months in the company of Ramana Maharshi. It is during this period that Maharshi's influence made its profound impact on Ramsurat. One day while meditating in the Master's presence he felt an intense attention being placed upon him; when he looked up, he saw Ramana Maharshi gazing at him. The experience was one of being transported outside of time and space entirely; he felt all previous and future lives coexisting and knew this was the onset of a complete internal transformation.

Soon after, Ramsurat once again decided to visit Papa Ramdas. He journeyed to Kerala and found, as before, that he felt no connection with this Master, so he headed north to wander in the Himalayas, seeking the company of great saints, gurus and adepts. While in the mountains he received news of the passing of Ramana Maharshi, and following close on its heels he heard also of the passing of Sri Aurobindo; both major influences in his quest were suddenly physically gone. It was this tremendous shock which sent him once again, in 1952, south to Kanhangad, Kerala, and Swami Papa Ramdas.

"This time," Yogi Ramsuratkumar recalled, "Swami Ramdas turned out to be an entirely different person. At the very first sight, Ramdas could tell a number of intimate things about the life and mission of this beggar which nobody but this beggar knew. Not only that but the Master started to take a special care of this beggar. This beggar began to feel from the environment of the ashram that Ramdas was a Sage, a truly great Sage. It was then that this beggar first understood the great Master, Ramdas, is this beggar's Father."[2]

In hindsight Yogi Ramsuratkumar felt that it was his Father, Ramdas, who had been preventing him from recognizing the intimate bond between them all along. The timing had to be just right, and now it was. He rapidly progressed, fed by his insatiable drive to tear away the veils which kept him from clearly seeing what he had always intuited as his mission in this lifetime. One day after witnessing the initiation of another devotee into the mantra, *Om Sri Ram Jai Ram Jai Jai Ram*, Ramsurat experienced a great urgency to be initiated himself. He approached Ramdas who looked aside for a moment, then focused on Ramsurat and declared with a smile, "So you want to be initiated? Sit down!"[3]

Afterwards, he repeated the mantra twenty-four hours a day, dancing and delighting in higher and clearer visions of a life in God. The internal transformation was completing itself and Yogi Ramsuratkumar's love for his father grew ever larger, until soon he could not stand to be without his father's company and Ramdas found it necessary to request Yogi Ramsuratkumar to leave. When asked where he would go, Yogi Ramsuratkumar without hesitation replied, "Arunachala," and after making one last journey around Mother India, he arrived there seven years later, never to leave again.

Yogi Ramsuratkumar has insisted that he is not a guru, and not because of the *Advaitic* (non-dual) reasoning used by other sages, but because he insistently remains a Beggar, both literally and

---

2 Wadlington, Truman Caylor. *Yogi Ramsuratkumar—The Godchild of Tiruvannamalai*, p. 40-41 (Diocesan Press, Madras, India, 1979).

3 Ibid, p. 55.

metaphorically. Dressed in rags and holding only a country hand-fan and a coconut begging bowl, he stretches forth his hand, palm out, and showers his Father's blessings on all who approach him, entreating each one to remember Ram's name, the Divine name, always and without fail. His devotees have recognized in him an incarnation of Ram, who spreads his *darbar*, the spiritual influence of his royal court, throughout the world.

Yogi Ramsuratkumar asks us to be compassionate, to treat everyone with kindness and respect; he calls the world to honor and keep the ancient tradition of begging alive in India as an example of a culture which embraces this ideal of human kindness. There are many in India who shun the spiritual heritage of their country, who have identified with Western values and seek a rational, scientific perspective of life, but Yogi Ramsuratkumar teaches that India's spiritual heritage should never be abandoned in favor of so-called modern life. His vision is for Mother India to remain the rich and fertile ground which gives birth to the profound wisdom and spiritual nourishment that has nurtured the world and her peoples for thousands of years.

Although flamboyant miracles do not seem to be part of Yogi Ramsuratkumar's mission, many of his devotees enthusiastically proclaim that the miraculous is at work in their lives through the blessing and spiritual influence of Yogi Ramsuratkumar. Once when a school girl, the daughter of a devotee, approached and told how her school teacher had taught that only God in the sky can perform miracles, that human beings like yogis never could, Yogi Ramsuratkumar smiled and had her hold a stainless steel plate up over a burning candle. From across the room he raised his hand and sent *shaktipat* towards the plate and when told to look, the girl saw the Yogi's image clearly and distinctly outlined in the soot left by the candle. He told her, "Go tell your teacher that God in the sky is not the only one who can perform miracles. God on earth can too!"

As the numbers of devotees of the self-proclaimed Crazy Sinner, the Godchild of Tiruvannamalai, have swelled into the tens and hundreds of thousands, celebrations are now held in various cities and villages across Southern India on his *jayanthi,* or birthday. The demand for a residence that can meet the growing needs of Yogi Ramsuratkumar and his teaching work have become more urgent, and so the construction of a permanent ashram in Tiruvannamalai was begun in 1994. In 1993 Ma Devaki, a devoted disciple, joined Yogi Ramsuratkumar as his attendant, caring for the Master's daily needs and assisting with the constant stream of devotees who come for the Master's *darshan.*

In 1991 the construction of a temple, the Manthralayam, near Kanyakumari, on the southernmost tip of India, was initiated, which was completed and formally inaugurated in September, 1993. The Manthralayam, where a 14-foot high stone *murti,* or spiritually empowered statue of Yogi Ramsuratkumar has been enshrined, has received the Yogi's full support and blessings; several times each day a brahmin priest performs the traditional *Vedic* rites before the *murti* of the Master. Every year Yogi Ramsuratkumar's *jayanthi* will be celebrated at the Manthralayam, while Yogi Ramsuratkumar's name is chanted continuously for several days, along with the mantra, *Om Sri Ram Jai Ram Jai Jai Ram.*

Yogi Ramsuratkumar has recently alluded to the fact that the time has come for him to emerge fully from his years of self-imposed seclusion and relative anonymity to enter the world arena as a spiritual force. When someone writes something in praise of the Mad Beggar, he heaps gratitude upon the author and says the person has done wonderful service. Lee Lozowick, an ardent American devotee, has written hundreds of poems to the Beggar, sending them through the mail one after the other. These poems are written in the traditional style of the devotee speaking in praise of his *Ishta Devataa,* or chosen Deity, the human embodiment of the Divine. Any devotees or visitors who may be present to receive the *darshan* of Yogi Ramsuratkumar are likely to hear him ask his attendant, Ma Devaki, to read these devotional poems again and again while he weeps and laughs in childlike embarrassment, delight and joy.

The universal mission with which he has been entrusted is evolving steadily, and he has remarked that if we were to suddenly fall into a deep sleep lasting 25 years we would wake to a totally transformed and glorious world. Sri Yogi Ramsuratkumar is the Eternal Beggar, ever bowing at the Feet of God in supplication for the well-being and continued transformation of God's Creation, and so his every gesture is embued with divine presence. Paradoxically, his universal work goes on essentially independent of those who are his devotees, as there are many who come seeking personal fulfillment, health, wealth, or even miracles.

However, one has the opportunity to recognize a different role in Sri Yogi Ramsuratkumar; indeed, it is the divine mood, the Heart of the Master, which plunges his devotees into profound longing for the Beloved. His glance penetrates to the depths of the human heart. The ultimate benediction which the Godchild of Tiruvannamalai bestows upon the human heart—when one is truly willing—is complete consummation in the fire of God's Love.